Environmental Assessment for
Proposed Restoration Activities on the

Sacramento River
National Wildlife Refuge

Ryan, Ohm, Haleakala, Pine Creek, Kaiser, Phelan Island, Koehnen, Hartley Island, and Stone Units

U.S. Fish and Wildlife Service
Sacramento River National Wildlife Refuge
Willows, California

Prepared by:

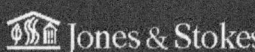 Jones & Stokes

May 2001

PROPOSED FINDING OF NO SIGNIFICANT IMPACT

PROPOSED RESTORATION ACTIVITIES ON THE
RYAN, OHM, HALEAKALA, PINE CREEK, KAISER, PHELAN ISLAND, KOEHNEN, HARTLEY ISLAND, AND STONE UNITS

SACRAMENTO RIVER NATIONAL WILDLIFE REFUGE

Sacramento National Wildlife Refuge Complex
752 County Road 99W, Willows, CA 95988

The U.S. Fish and Wildlife Service (Service) proposes to reestablish or enhance native riparian vegetation on lands within the Sacramento River National Wildlife Refuge (SRNWR) owned (in fee title) by the Service. Approximately 2,372 acres of land on 11 existing units or subunits within the SRNWR will be planted or allowed to revegetate with native vegetation as a result of the proposed action. These efforts will focus on restoring or enhancing natural vegetation communities that have been converted to agricultural and other uses in the past. After adequate planning, orchards and other crops will be removed along with most of the related infrastructure (remnant, nonfunctional farming facilities such as pumping units, barns, and sheds). To accomplish restoration, native species will then be planted and actively maintained for several years. Over time, habitat management and natural processes will control the species composition and overall structure of the plant communities. The restoration sites are along the Sacramento River from river mile (RM) 240 downstream to RM 164 on the Ryan, Ohm, Haleakala, Pine Creek, Kaiser, Phelan Island, Koehnen, Hartley Island, and Stone units of the refuge. Slightly more than 37% of these lands currently supports riparian vegetation. Over the next 5–10 years, an additional 60% (approximately 2,372 acres) of the lands will be planted with native riparian vegetation; the remaining 3% of the project area will remain in water surface, gravel bars, and other unvegetated land. This revegetation will require removal of 2,372 acres of primarily agricultural land and the planting of a mix of habitat types. Benefits of this action include:
- preservation, restoration, and enhancement, in their natural ecosystems, all species of animals and plants relying on riparian habitat in the Sacramento Valley that are endangered or threatened with becoming endangered;
- perpetuation of the migratory bird resource;
- preservation of natural diversity and abundance of fauna and flora on refuge lands; and
- providing an understanding and appreciation of fish and wildlife ecology as well as human roles in the environment.

The Service has analyzed the following alternatives to the proposal. The no action alternative was analyzed and found to be inadequate because it did not to meet the objectives of the proposed action. Riparian vegetation would not be restored or enhanced on the existing SRNWR lands. Conditions on these properties would remain the same, with some acreage supporting native or replanted riparian habitat and other acreage continuing with agricultural operations. There would be neither positive nor negative direct effects on the refuge lands.

Without active revegetation efforts, there would be no near-term benefit to wildlife and vegetation.

The Service has considered a number of alternative planting programs for the project units. To hasten the development of the habitat, the Service considered removal of existing crops as soon as parcels were purchased and funds were available to implement the planting. This alternative would not take advantage of the remaining productive life of the orchard crops on the parcels. Alternative planting patterns and densities have also been considered. The creation of primarily dense riparian forest has been considered for all units. However, using soils information and (in some cases) hydrologic modeling, the Service is selecting planting patterns that offer the best opportunity for long-term vegetation success without risking substantial changes in local hydrology.

The Service has also considered the alternative of allowing passive revegetation of its refuge units. This alternative was not pursued because it would have no short-term value to wildlife. Also, recruitment would likely include many nonnative species with lower value to the target wildlife species.

The Service did not consider alternative locations for restoration of habitat. The lands considered in this EA are already part of the SRNWR. During the acquisition process, the Service used a number of selection criteria to identify parcels for restoration, including biological significance of each tract, existing and anticipated threats to the tract's wildlife value, and landowner's willingness to sell the property.

The proposed action was selected because it will fulfill the Service's congressional mandate to preserve, restore, and enhance riparian habitat for threatened and endangered species, songbirds, waterfowl, other migratory birds, anadromous fish, resident riparian wildlife, and plants. To meet this purpose, any action must, by definition, include the addition and protection of habitat along the Sacramento River. The primary factor used to differentiate the alternatives was the ability to achieve the purpose of habitat restoration while possibly reducing the potential adverse effects of the proposed action. The proposed action met the objectives of the habitat restoration efforts without increasing the adverse environmental and socioeconomic effects.

Implementation of the proposed action would be expected to result in the following environmental effects:
- Beneficial impact: Special-status plants and sensitive natural communities would benefit from the increase in acreage of forest, scrub, savannah, grassland, and wetland communities throughout the SRNWR.
- Beneficial impact: Management to promote greater species diversity, protection from adjacent land uses, and an areal increase of natural communities.
- Beneficial impact: Long-term beneficial effects on fish in the Sacramento River. This project will contribute complexity to the aquatic environment, providing cover, food, and other habitat components for fish.

2

- Potential impacts on giant garter snake habitat during restoration activities.
- Potential impacts on water quality due to increased sedimentation.
- Potential impacts on buried cultural artifacts during restoration activities.

Measures to mitigate and/or minimize adverse effects have been implemented into the proposed action and include:

- **Mitigation Measure 4.3.2-1: Avoid Giant Garter Snake Habitat by Restricting Location and Timing of Project Activities.** If project activities will take place within 200 feet of potential habitat between April 1 and October 1, surveys will be conducted immediately prior to ground disturbance. No ground-disturbing activities will occur within 200 feet of potential habitat from October 1 through April 1 without consulting with the Service.

- **Mitigation Measure 4.3.3-1: Implement Best Management Practices to Avoid Reduction in Water Quality.** Best management practices (BMPs) could include a variety of sediment control measures such as silt fences, straw or rice bale barriers, brush or rock filters, sediment traps, fiber rolls, or other similar linear barriers that can be placed at the edge of the project area to prevent sediment from flowing off site. The exact location and placement of the various sediment control BMPs will be determined by the individual responsible for implementing the SWPPP in accordance with changing site conditions. The contractor will establish a spill prevention and countermeasure plan before project construction begins; this plan will include on-site handling criteria to avoid input of contaminants to the waterway. A staging, washing, and storage area will be provided away from the waterway for equipment, construction materials, fuels, lubricants, solvents, and other possible contaminants.

- **Mitigation Measure 4.4.6-1: Conduct a Cultural Resources Investigation that Includes Pedestrian Survey and Recordation of Resources.** Before activities that could affect cultural resources occur on these parcels, a formal cultural resources inventory should be performed by qualified cultural resources specialists. This inventory should include a records search, a pedestrian survey, and an inventory report. A qualified archaeologist, in consultation with refuge staff and the Service's cultural resources division, can decide if an update to the records search performed by Jones & Stokes in January 2001 at the Northeast Information Center of the California Historical Information System at California State University, Chico, is necessary. It is recommended that the intensive pedestrian survey of areas determined by a qualified archaeologist to be sensitive for the presence of cultural resources be conducted with 15 meters or less between survey transects. Identified cultural resources must be formally documented. Consultation with the native American community will be necessary to ensure identification of traditional cultural properties. A qualified architectural historian may be needed to record and evaluate project effects on extant historic buildings and structures. The results of this inventory should be presented in a cultural resources inventory report. The report should include recommendations, developed in consultation with the State Historic Preservation Officer (SHPO), for procedures to avoid significant effects on cultural resources.

- **Mitigation Measure 4.4.6-2: Stop Work if Buried Cultural Resources Are Inadvertently Discovered during Ground-Disturbing Activities and Assess Significance of the Resources.** If buried cultural resources, such as chipped or ground stone, midden soil,

3

or historic debris, are inadvertently discovered during ground-disturbing activities, work will stop in that area and within 100 feet of the find until a qualified archaeologist can assess the significance of the find and, if necessary, develop appropriate treatment measures in consultation with the SHPO and other appropriate agencies.

- **Mitigation Measure 4.4.6-3: Comply with Federal Laws Pertaining to the Discovery of Human Remains.** If human remains are discovered during project activities, the county coroner or sheriff should be called to determine if the remains are of native American origin. When human remains are discovered on federal land and determined to be of native American origin, the responsible federal agency is required to comply with requirements of the Native American Graves Protection and Repatriation Act (NAGPRA) (see Chapter 5). The regulations implementing the requirements of NAGPRA relating to the inadvertent discovery of human remains of native American origin are described in 43 CFR, Part 10, Subpart B, Section 10.4. and include the following provisions, which should be implemented by the Service:
    - cease activity in the area of discovery and protect the human remains;
    - take steps to secure and protect the human remains;
    - notify the Indian tribe or tribes likely to be culturally affiliated with the discovered human remains within 1 working day; and
    - initiate consultation with the Indian tribe or tribes in accordance with regulations described in 43 CFR, Part 10, Subpart B, Section 10.5.

The proposed project is not expected to have any significant effects on the human environment because all environmental impacts have either been eliminated through project design or the mitigation implemented would reduce impacts to a less-than-significant level.

The proposed project has been or will be thoroughly coordinated with all interested and/or affected parties including:
- Sacramento River Conservation Area
- Sacramento River Preservation Trust
- California Department of Fish and Game
- The Reclamation Board
- The Nature Conservancy
- U.S. Fish and Wildlife Service
- National Marine Fisheries Service
- U.S. Army Corps of Engineers
- California Department of Water Resources
- Tehama, Butte and Glenn Counties
- Central Valley Branch of the Regional Water Quality Control Board
- State of California, Office of Historic Preservation

Public Availability: This preliminary finding of no significant impact and the supporting environmental assessment are available for public review and comment for the 45-day period specified in the cover letter transmitting this document. This document has been distributed to

Federal, State, and local agencies; public libraries; potentially affected landowners; and private groups and individuals upon their request. Additional copies are available from:

U.S. Fish and Wildlife Service
Sacramento National Wildlife Refuge Complex
752 County Road 99W
Willows, CA 95988
Phone 530-934-2801

Based on information contained in this environmental assessment, it is my preliminary determination that the proposed action does not constitute a major federal action significantly affecting the quality of the human environment. As such, an environmental impact statement is not required. The attached environmental assessment has been prepared in support of this preliminary finding.

Reference: Proposed restoration activities on the Ryan, Ohm, Haleakala, Pine Creek, Kaiser, Phelan Island, Koehnen, Hartley Island, and Stone Units

ENVIRONMENTAL ASSESSMENT

Proposed Restoration Activities on the Sacramento River National Wildlife Refuge

(Ryan, Ohm, Haleakala, Pine Creek, Kaiser, Phelan Island, Koehnen, Hartley Island, and Stone Units)

Prepared for:

Department of the Interior
U.S. Fish and Wildlife Service
Sacramento River National Wildlife Refuge
752 County Road 99W
Willows, CA 95988
Contacts: Kevin Foerster and Ramon Vega

Prepared by:

Jones & Stokes
2600 V Street
Sacramento, CA 95818-1914
Contacts: Mike Rushton and Karen Shaffer
916/503-6681

Under Contract to:

The Nature Conservancy
Sacramento, CA

May 2001

U.S. Fish and Wildlife Service. 2001. Environmental assessment for proposed restoration activities on the Sacramento River National Wildlife Refuge. May. Willows, CA. Prepared by Jones & Stokes, Sacramento, CA.

TABLE OF CONTENTS

LIST OF TABLES

LIST OF FIGURES

CHAPTER 1. PURPOSE OF AND NEED FOR THE PROPOSED ACTION

1.1 BACKGROUND

This environmental assessment (EA) has been prepared to assist the U.S. Fish and Wildlife Service (Service) in developing habitat enhancement and restoration activities within the approved boundary of the Sacramento River National Wildlife Refuge (SRNWR). The EA will serve as a vehicle to provide information to and solicit input from the general public during the planning process, and will be used in the decision-making process. Because the actions evaluated in this document will occur on federal property, could be fully or partially funded by federal agencies, and will require federal permits and approvals, environmental documentation under the National Environmental Policy Act (NEPA) is required. The EA addresses direct, indirect, and cumulative effects of the proposed habitat enhancement and restoration activities that can be identified without undue speculation. These effects are considered in the context of specific locations where appropriate and in a broader, project-wide or cumulative sense where the overall impact is more relevant.

The geographical scope of the EA encompasses the area along the Sacramento River between Red Bluff and north of Princeton in Tehama, Butte, and Glenn Counties, California, as authorized by Congress in the Middle Sacramento River Refuge Feasibility Study (U.S. Fish and Wildlife Service 1987) and identified in the Environmental Assessment and Finding of No Significant Impact for the Proposed Sacramento River National Wildlife Refuge (U.S. Fish and Wildlife Service 1989). The latter document established and authorized the acquisition of up to 18,000 acres for the refuge in Butte, Tehama, Glenn, and Colusa Counties.

This EA addresses only habitat enhancement and restoration activities in the SRNWR and is not intended to provide in-depth discussions of related issues of concern, such as public use. Public use opportunities will be planned and evaluated during the development of a Comprehensive Conservation Plan (CCP) for the SRNWR. The CCP will be initiated in April 2001 and will address all public use activities on the refuge, including hunting, fishing, wildlife observation, photography, environmental education, and interpretation, for a 15-year period. The development of the CCP was mandated by Congress with the passage of the National Wildlife Refuge System Improvement Act of 1997 (16 USC 668).

The proposed action will be implemented within a nationwide system of federal refuges and in accordance with the overall mission of the National Wildlife Refuge System (Refuge System). This mission is to administer a national network of lands and waters for the conservation, management, and restoration of fish, wildlife, and plant resources and their habitats in the United States for the benefit of present and future generations of Americans (National Wildlife Refuge System Improvement Act of 1997). The Refuge System is a network of protected lands and waters dedicated for fish and wildlife. Since the Refuge System's inception in 1903 with the establishment of Pelican Island National Wildlife Refuge in Florida, the Refuge System has grown to more than 530 refuges, with at least one refuge in every state. California has 40 national wildlife refuges covering more than 444,000 acres.

1.2 PURPOSE OF THE PROPOSED ACTION

The purpose of enhancing and restoring riparian and associated habitats within the SRNWR (the proposed action being evaluated in this EA) is to help fulfill the Service's congressional mandate to preserve, restore, and enhance riparian habitat for threatened and endangered species, songbirds, waterfowl, other migratory birds, anadromous fish, resident riparian wildlife, and plants.

In addition, the following broad goals of the Refuge System describe a level of responsibility and concern for the nation's wildlife resources for the ultimate benefit of people:

- to preserve, restore, and enhance in their natural ecosystems all species of animals and plants that are endangered or threatened with becoming endangered;

- to perpetuate the migratory bird resource;

- to preserve a natural diversity and abundance of fauna and flora on refuge lands;

- to provide an understanding and appreciation of fish and wildlife ecology as well as human roles in the environment, and to provide refuge visitors with high-quality, safe, wholesome, and enjoyable recreational experiences oriented toward wildlife to the extent that these activities are compatible with the purposes for which the refuge was established.

1.3 NEED FOR THE PROPOSED ACTION

Historically, 500,000 acres of riparian forests occupied the Sacramento River floodplain, with valley oak woodland covering the higher river terraces. Use of trees for lumber and fuel, particularly cordwood for steamboats, reduced the extent of the riparian forests in the Sacramento Valley during the late 1800s. Since then, urbanization and agricultural conversion have been the primary factors in eliminating riparian habitat. Water development and reclamation projects, including channelization, dam and levee construction, bank protection, and streamflow regulation, have altered the riparian system and contributed to vegetation loss. Riparian vegetation along the Sacramento River and its tributaries has been reduced by approximately 89% in the last 100–120 years. Riparian habitat along the Sacramento River is critically important for various threatened and endangered species, neotropical migrants, waterfowl and other migratory birds, anadromous fish, native wildlife, and plants.

CHAPTER 2. DESCRIPTION OF THE PROPOSED ACTION AND ALTERNATIVES

2.1 INTRODUCTION

This chapter presents the proposed action and alternatives to the proposed action, including the no action alternative. NEPA requires analysis at the EA level of project alternatives that would avoid or minimize potential environmental impacts. The alternatives analyzed in this EA include the proposed action and Alternative 1, the no action alternative. The objectives of the proposed action are to reestablish or enhance native riparian vegetation on units of the SRNWR owned by the Service. Under Alternative 1, no restoration activities would take place and any increase in native vegetation would be through natural revegetation. Two other alternatives are considered; Alternative 2 would minimize hydrologic effects of the proposed action, and Alternative 3 would minimize conversion of prime farmland (as designated by the State Department of Conservation and the Natural Resources Conservation Service [NRCS]) that would be associated with the proposed action. One other alternative was considered but dismissed because it did not meet the objectives of the proposed action and, in the long term, had the potential to cause adverse environmental impacts equal to or greater than those of the proposed action.

2.2 PROPOSED ACTION

2.2.1 Overview of the Proposed Action

The proposed action is the reestablishment or enhancement of native riparian vegetation on lands within the SRNWR owned (in fee title) by the Service. Approximately 2,372 acres of land on eleven existing units or subunits within the SRNWR will be planted or allowed to revegetate with native vegetation as a result of the proposed action (Figure 1 and Table 2-1).

2.2.2 Location and Description of Project Area

The SRNWR is located along the Sacramento River within the Sacramento Valley of California. The proposed action's restoration and enhancement sites are distributed along approximately 76 river miles within Glenn, Butte, and Tehama Counties.

The SRNWR is part of the Sacramento National Wildlife Refuge complex, consisting of six refuges and three wildlife management areas within the Sacramento Valley. The SRNWR is currently composed of 19 units between the cities of Red Bluff and Princeton, from river miles (RMs) 240 to 164 (Figure 1). Congress authorized the Service to develop an 18,000-acre SRNWR; to date approximately 11,215 acres (including 1,280 acres under a riparian conservation easement) have been acquired. Some of the acquired acreage has been restored, and additional acres are planned for restoration. Approximately 40% of the existing refuge acreage is under agricultural production—primarily walnut, almond, and prune orchards and field crops. The remaining acreage is composed primarily of riparian habitat, wetlands, and uplands in Tehama, Butte, and Glenn Counties.

2.2.3 Proposed Revegetation of Existing SRNWR Lands

The Service will revegetate existing lands within the SRNWR to restore and enhance the natural ecosystems of the Sacramento River. These efforts will focus on restoring or enhancing natural vegetation communities that have been converted to agricultural and other uses in the past. After adequate planning, orchards and other crops will be removed along with most of the related infrastructure (remnant, nonfunctional farming facilities such as pumping units, barns, and sheds). To accomplish restoration, native species will then be planted and actively maintained for several years. Over time, habitat management and natural processes will control the species composition and overall structure of the plant communities.

The restoration sites are along the river from RM 240 downstream to RM 164 on the Ryan, Ohm, Haleakala, Pine Creek, Kaiser, Phelan Island, Koehnen, Hartley Island, and Stone units of the refuge (Figure 2). Slightly more than 37% of these lands currently supports riparian vegetation. Over the next 5–10 years, an additional 60% (approximately 2,372 acres) of the lands will be planted with native riparian vegetation; the remaining 3% of the project area will remain in water surface, gravel bars, and other unvegetated land. This revegetation will require removal of 2,372 acres of primarily agricultural land and the planting of a mix of habitat types.

2.2.4 Generalized Restoration Program

Figure 3 illustrates the general process followed for any restoration project within the SRNWR. The restoration and habitat management steps are site planning, site preparation, installation and planting, maintenance, and monitoring.

The first step is site planning, where site-specific information (e.g., background studies on geomorphology, vegetation structure and wildlife, soils, hydrology, cultural resources) is collected and a detailed restoration design is developed. The restoration design includes which species will be planted, at what density, and in what pattern. A document called a unit plan is the result of the site planning actions for many of the restoration projects. Site planning can take up to 2 years to complete.

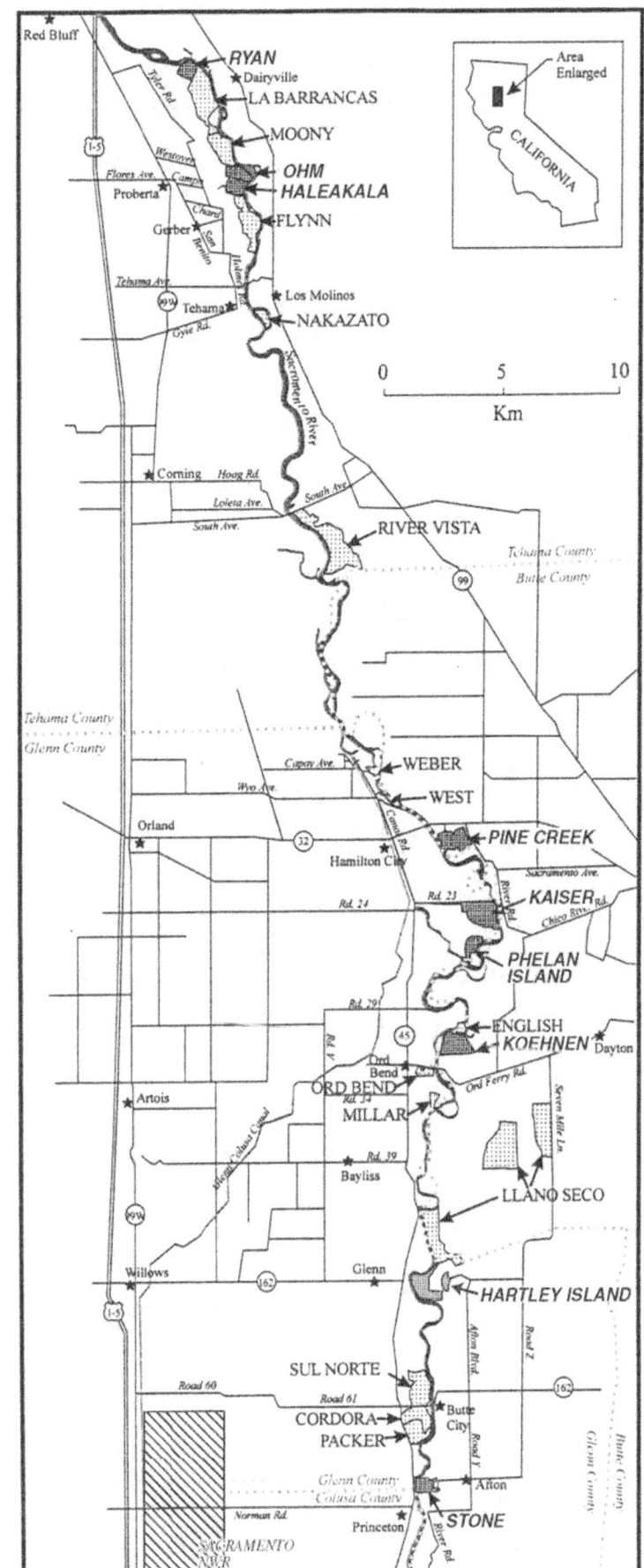

🏛 Jones & Stokes

Figure 1
Sacramento River National Wildlife Refuge – Unit Locations

Table 2-1. Proposed Riparian Restoration/Enhancement Program for Existing SRNWR Units

Unit/ Subunit	River Mile	County	Current Ownership	Total Acres	Current Agricultural Acres	Current Crop	Estimated Remaining Orchard Life	Estimated Year of Restoration	Acres Available for Restoration	Restoration Priority
Ryan	240–240.5	Tehama	Refuge	247	47	walnuts	2–3 years	2002–4	47	medium
Ohm	234–235	Tehama	Refuge	500		open field		2002–4	100	medium
Haleakala	233–233.5	Tehama	Refuge	250	206	walnuts	2–5 years	2003–5	206	high
Pine Creek	196–199	Butte	Refuge	347	85	walnuts	5–7 years	2005–7	85	medium
Harley	198.5–199.5	Butte	TNC – being transferred to refuge	103	20 / 72	walnuts / prunes	2–5 years	2002–4	92	high / high
Sunset Ranch	198–199	Butte	TNC – being transferred to refuge	100	6	walnuts / open field		2001–3	92	high
Kaiser	193–194	Glenn	Refuge	681		open field		2001–3	600	high
Phelan Island	191–192	Glenn	Refuge	279		open field		2001–3	62	high
Koehnen	186–186.5	Butte	Refuge	637	553	almonds / walnuts	2–3 years	2002–4	553	medium
Hartley Island	173–175	Glenn	Refuge	485	242 / 64	walnuts / prunes	5–10 years / 2–5 years	2003–5	306	medium
Stone	164.2–164.4	Glenn	Refuge	274		open field		2001–3	229	high
Total				3,903	1,295				2,372	

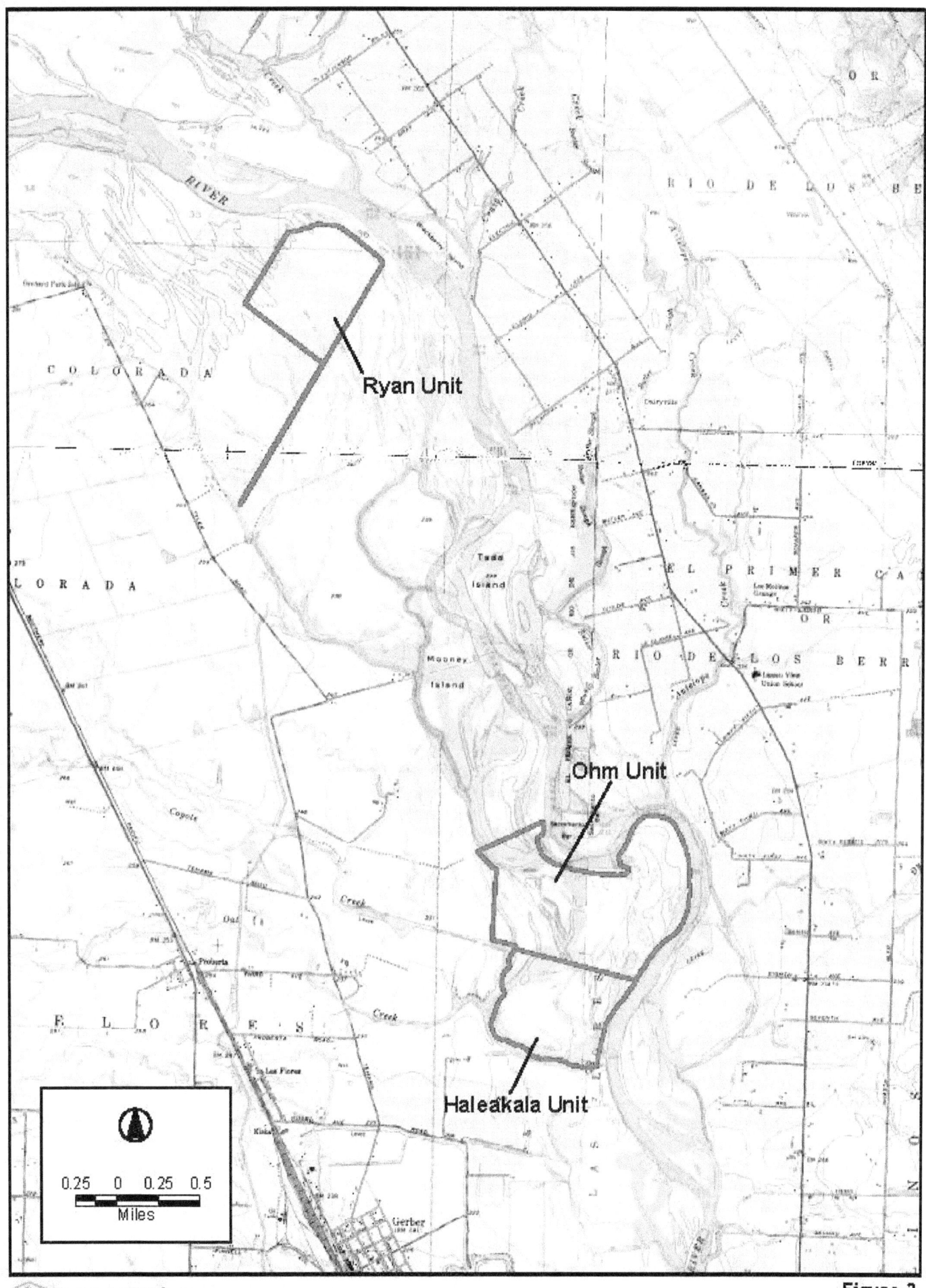

Ryan Unit

Ohm Unit

Haleakala Unit

Figure 2
SRNWR Units to be Restored (North to South)
Part 1 of 5

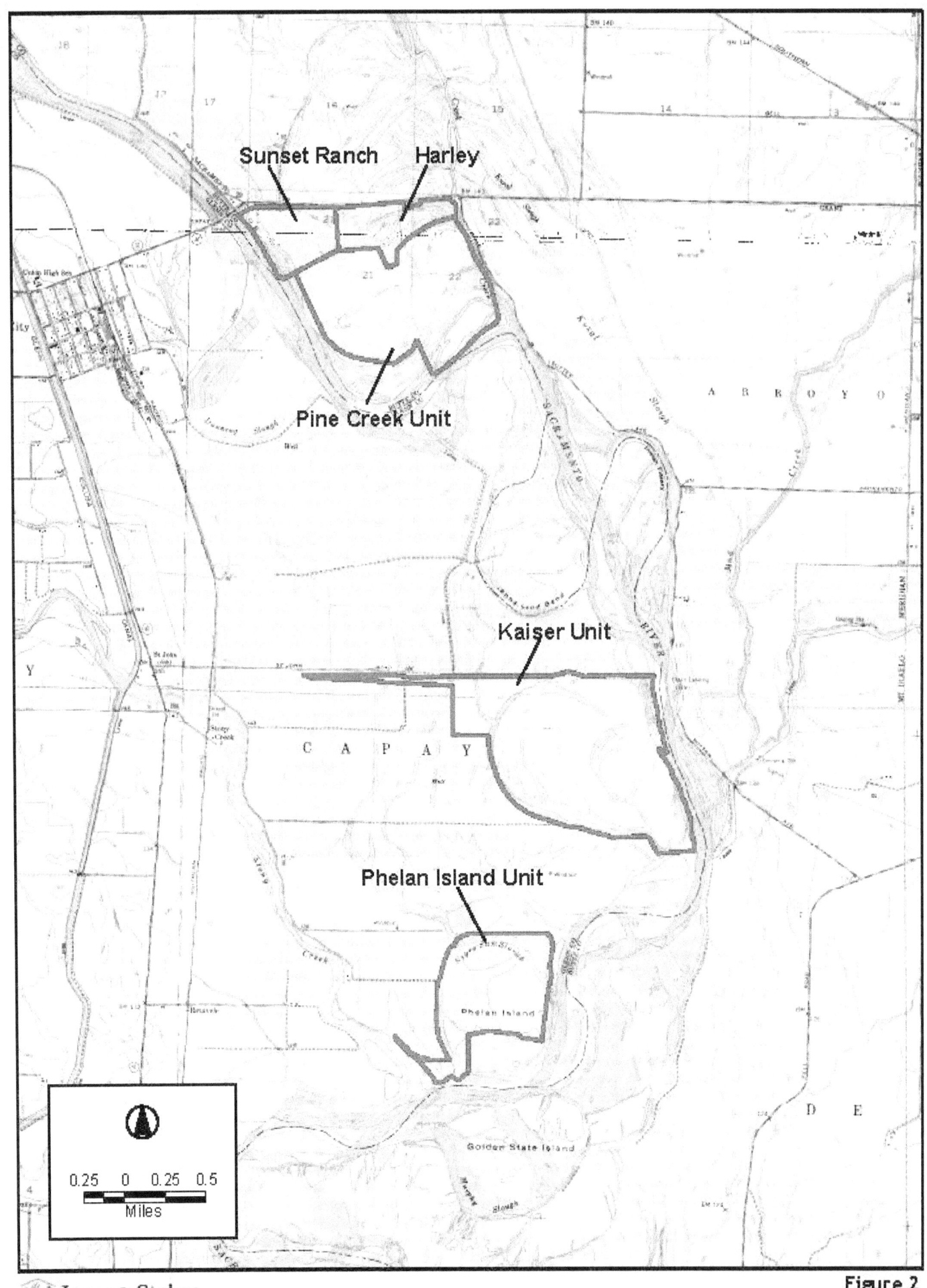

Sunset Ranch   Harley

Pine Creek Unit

Kaiser Unit

Phelan Island Unit

0.25   0   0.25   0.5
Miles

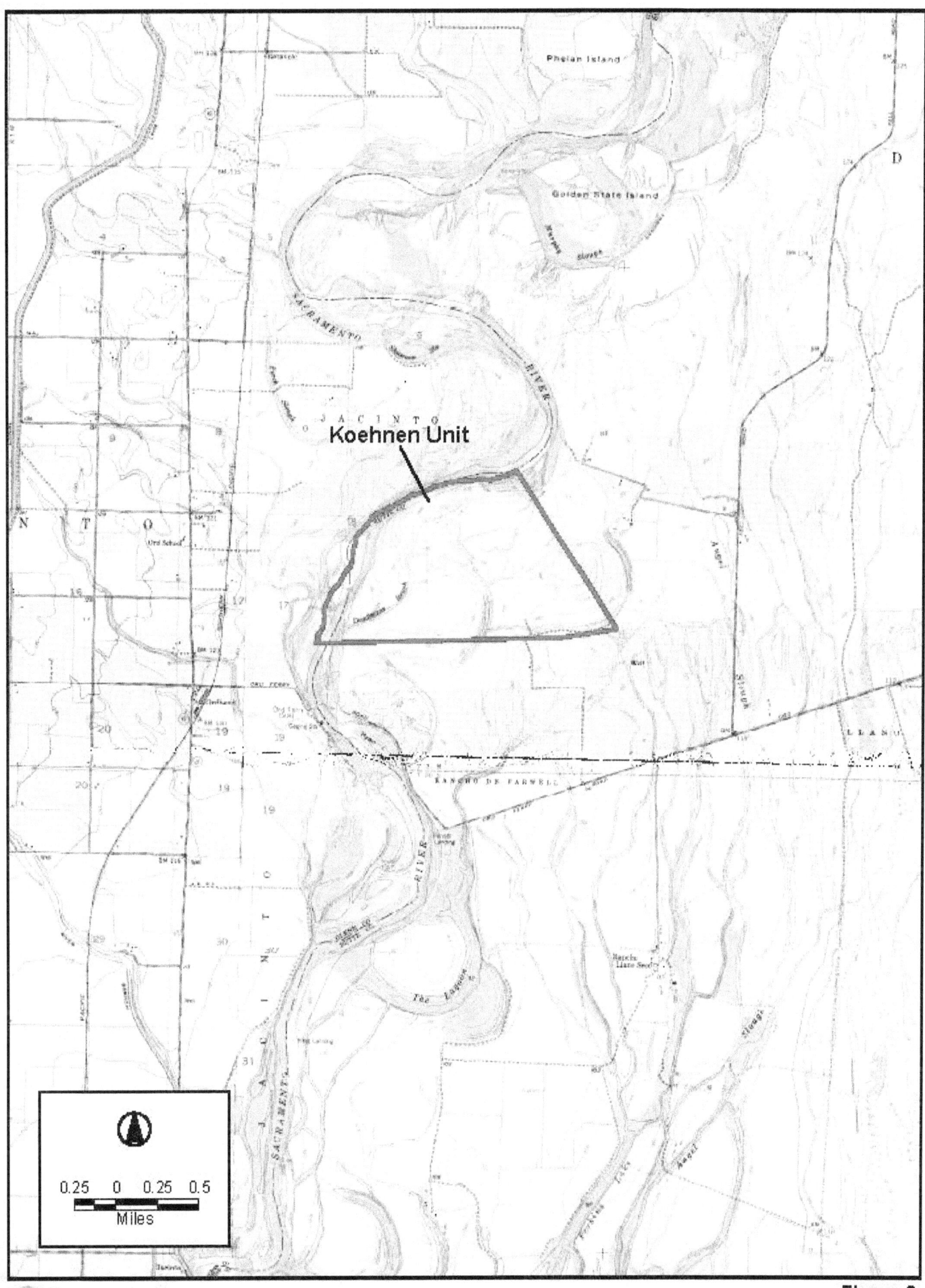

Koehnen Unit

0.25 0 0.25 0.5
Miles

Figure 2
SRNWR Units to be Restored (North to South)
Part 3 of 5

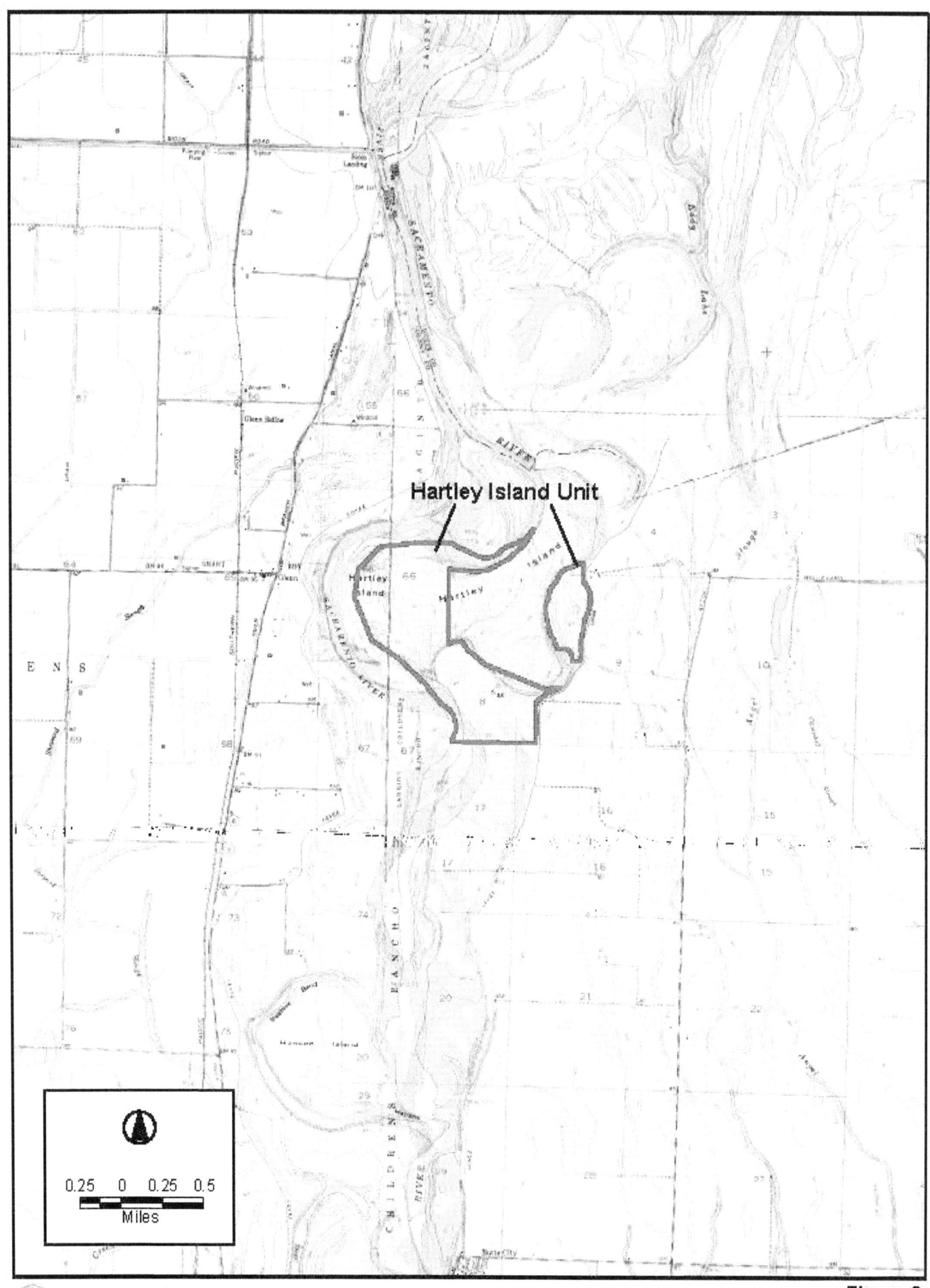

Hartley Island Unit

0.25 0 0.25 0.5
Miles

Figure 2
SRNWR Units to be Restored (North to South)
Part 4 of 5

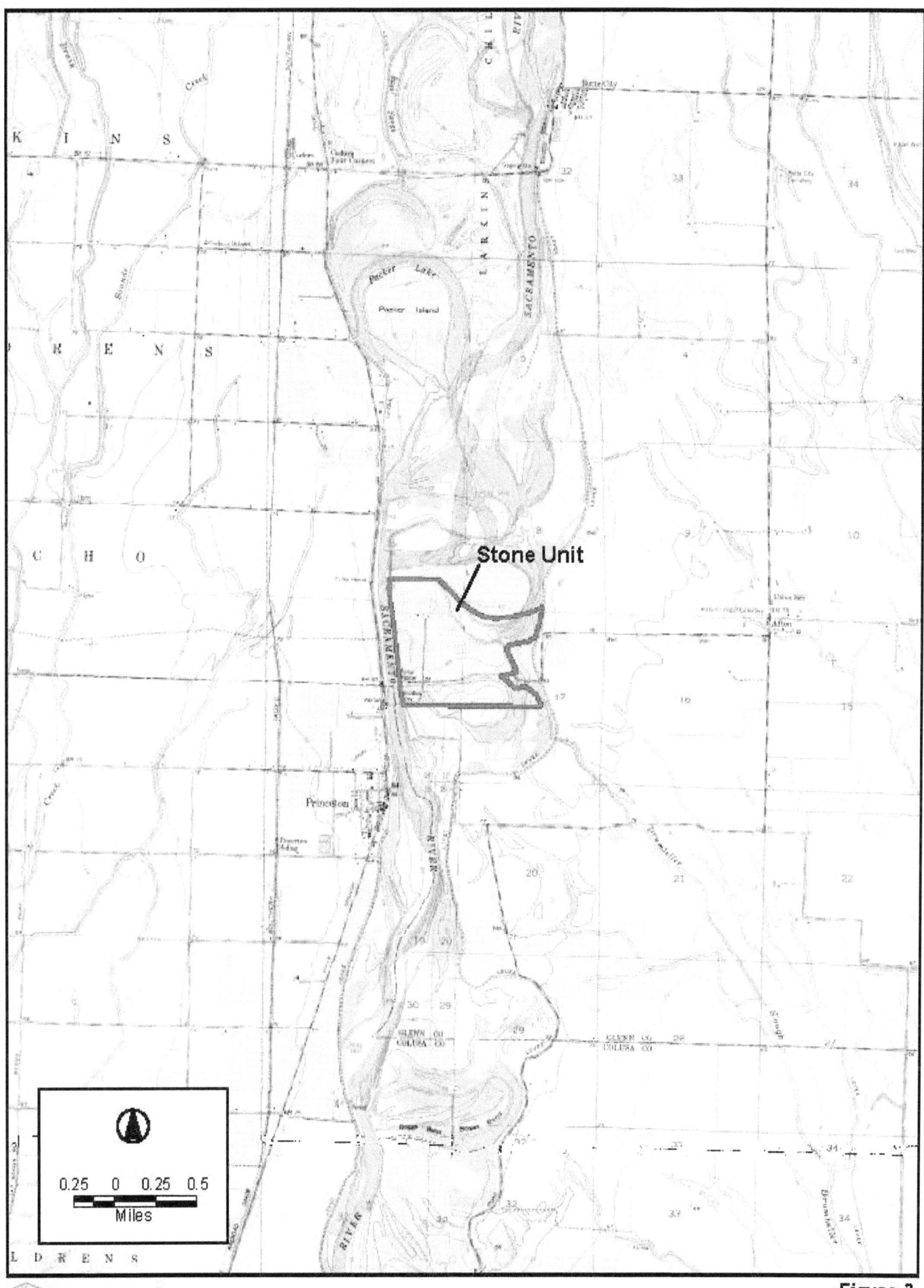

Stone Unit

Figure 2
SRNWR Units to be Restored (North to South)
Part 5 of 5

Figure 3. General Restoration Program for the SRNWR

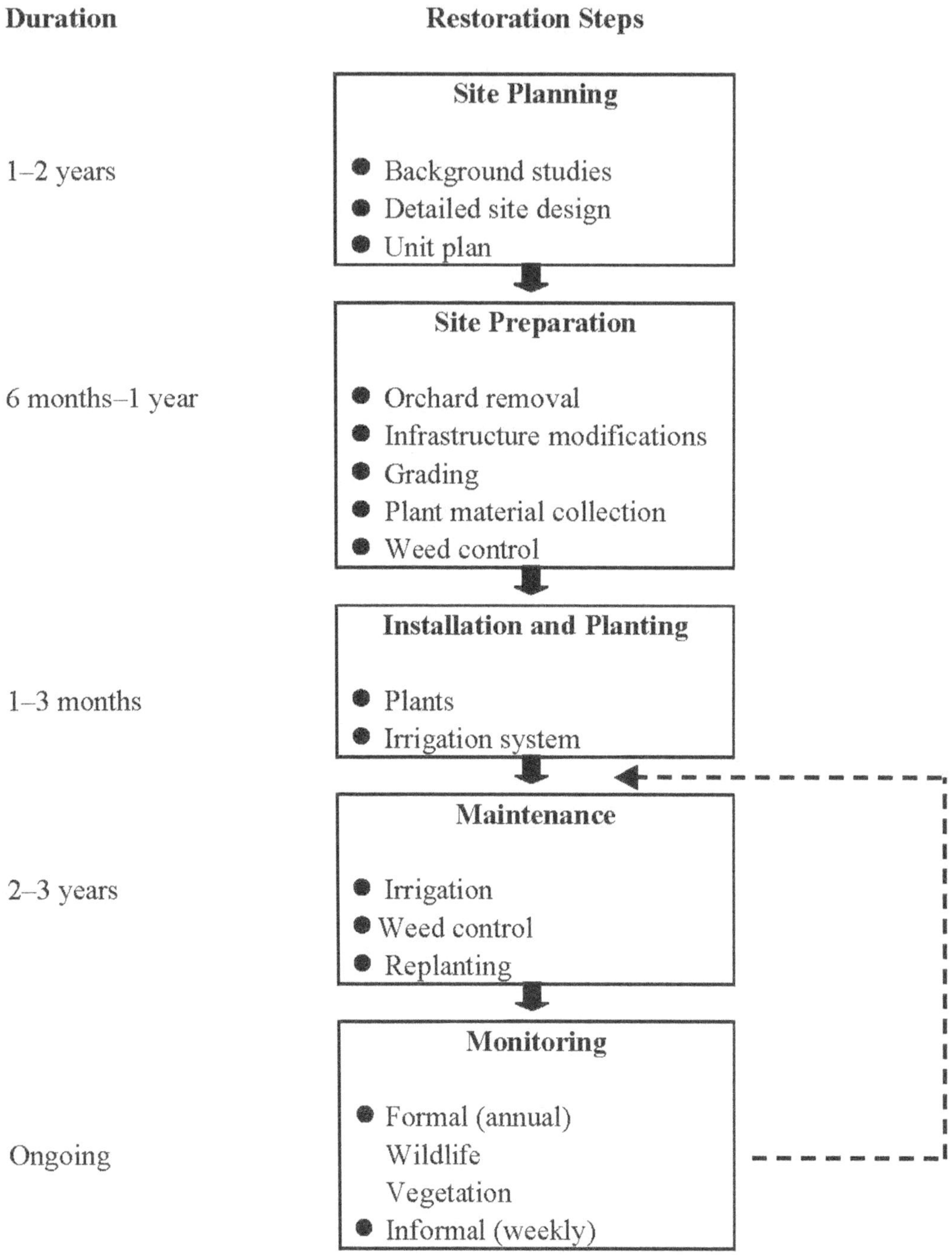

Duration	Restoration Steps

Duration

Restoration Steps

Site Planning

1–2 years

- Background studies
- Detailed site design
- Unit plan

Site Preparation

6 months–1 year

- Orchard removal
- Infrastructure modifications
- Grading
- Plant material collection
- Weed control

Installation and Planting

1–3 months

- Plants
- Irrigation system

Maintenance

2–3 years

- Irrigation
- Weed control
- Replanting

Monitoring

Ongoing

- Formal (annual)
  Wildlife
  Vegetation
- Informal (weekly)

The second step is site preparation, intended to make the site suitable for planting. Preparations can include orchard removal, infrastructure modification (i.e., removal of remnant, nonfunctional agricultural facilities), grading (limited to the level of normal farming activities), plant material collection, and weed control. The types of actions and the amount of work during site preparation will be specific to each project site. One site may require only a small quantity of weed control, whereas another may require an extensive amount of work for each type of preparation actions. These actions are consistent with accepted agricultural and refuge practices. Site preparation can take between 6 months and 1 year.

The third step is installation and planting. During this step the plant materials (i.e., cuttings, container stock, and seed stock such as acorns) are planted as specified in the unit plan. The irrigation system is installed, or the existing system modified, according to the unit plan. The irrigation system is typically a drip system; however, underground tape systems, solid set sprinkler systems, and flood irrigation may also be used. Installation and planting can take between 1 and 3 months.

The fourth step comprises maintenance activities. During this phase of the project, which typically lasts between 2 and 3 years, irrigation is continued as needed, weeds are controlled, and limited replanting may occur. Weed control can occur in a number of forms, including mowing, tilling, hand removal, prescribed fire, livestock grazing, and chemical control. Chemical control will be conducted in accordance with Service regulations. Maintenance activities are required as part of the site restoration to establish the plants.

The fifth step is monitoring. The survival and condition of plants in the restoration project are monitored. This monitoring is both formal and informal. Formal monitoring, conducted annually, focuses on survival. Informal monitoring is conducted weekly (or more frequently) and focuses on the conditions of the irrigation system, weeds, and status of the plants. Both types of monitoring are used to direct the follow-up actions. Monitoring will be ongoing.

As an adjunct to assessing the success of vegetative restoration, breeding birds are also monitored. This can entail methods such as fixed-radius point count, constant-effort mist netting, area nest searches, analysis of nesting vegetation, and fall migration monitoring. These data are used to analyze the status and trends of Sacramento River bird populations. Bird monitoring activities will be conducted by the Point Reyes Bird Observatory and refuge staff.

2.2.5 Restored Habitat Types and Related Restoration Actions

The habitat types that the proposed action is intended to restore are based on the classification systems of Holland (1986) and Sawyer and Keeler-Wolf (1995). Table 2-2 lists the Holland classifications and the dominant species associated with each community, and Appendix A contains a full description of each community. These habitat types should only be considered generally; the exact planting design for each project will be determined during site planning based on a detailed evaluation of specific site conditions. For this reason, each planting project will be unique in its details.

Communities in the Holland system can be categorized into three general types that have similar restoration actions. These three general types are forests, scrub, and savannas; grasslands; and associated wetlands.

Forest, Scrub, and Savanna Communities

Forest, scrub, and savanna communities are and will be the largest component of restored lands. They can be found throughout the Sacramento River floodplain and surrounding upland, depending on the local conditions. These communities are dominated by valley oak, Fremont cottonwood, willow species, western sycamore, and blue elderberry. Other species to be planted include Oregon ash, box elder, mule fat, California wild rose, coyote brush, white alder (*Alnus rhombifolia*), California blackberry (*Rubus vitifolius*), button-bush (*Cephalanthus occidentalis*), California wild grape (*Vitis californica*), and associated understory species. Planting methods include installation of cuttings, acorns, and nursery container stock. In many cases, little or no grading or topographic changes will be necessary. Weed control could include mowing, tilling, hand removal, burning, livestock grazing, and chemical control. Typically, one irrigation method is selected, such as drip, flood, or overhead sprinklers.

Grassland

Grassland communities will also be established within the SRNWR, particularly in areas where the soil cannot support riparian vegetation and in areas where riparian vegetation could pose a threat to flood control facilities. Species to be planted include wildrye (*Leymus triticoides*), blue wildrye (*Elymus glaucus*), purple needlegrass (*Nassella pulcra*), deergrass (*Matzlenbergia rigens*), Santa Barbara sedge (*Carex barbarae*), and meadow barley (*Hordeum brachyantherum*). Planting methods will include broadcast seeding and use of a seed drill. Frequently, little or no grading or topographic change will be necessary. Site preparation may require extensive efforts to control weeds. Weed control could include mowing, tilling, hand removal, burning, livestock grazing, and chemical control. If irrigation is required for this habitat type, overhead sprinklers are typically used.

Associated Wetlands

Associated wetlands can include backwater sloughs, oxbows, secondary channels, and topographic depressions. Earthmoving equipment may be required to construct these features or to reestablish historical flows to existing features. The revegetation methodology in these habitat types can be either recruitment (i.e., allowing plants to establish naturally over time) or cultivation (i.e., planting the desired species). Recruitment revegetation can be acceptable because of the high abundance of wetland seeds in the Sacramento River system and the short amount of time required for most species to reach maturity and begin producing seeds locally. If cultivated restoration is pursued, bulrush and cattails are likely to be planted along with other wetland species. Appendix B lists the common and scientific names of plant species mentioned in this EA.

Table 2-2. Holland Classification and Dominant Plant Species at SRNWR Units

Holland Classification	Dominant Species
Great Valley cottonwood riparian forest (Holland code 61410)	Cottonwood, willows
Great Valley mixed riparian forest (Holland code 61420)	Cottonwood, willows, sycamore, box elder, black walnut
Great Valley valley oak riparian forest (Holland code 61430)	Valley oak, sycamore, cottonwood, box elder
Great Valley willow scrub (Holland code 63410)	Willows
Coastal and valley freshwater marsh (Holland code 52410)	Bulrush, cattails

Note: See Appendix A for more complete descriptions of classifications.

2.3 Alternatives

2.3.1 Process Used to Develop the Alternatives

Alternatives to the proposed action were developed by reviewing the objectives of the habitat restoration efforts and identifying alternative ways to meet those objectives without increasing the adverse environmental and socioeconomic effects. As stated in Chapter 1, the purpose of the restoration efforts is to provide needed habitat for threatened and endangered species, songbirds, waterfowl and other migratory birds, anadromous fish, resident riparian wildlife, and plants. To meet this purpose, any action must, by definition, include the addition and protection of habitat along the Sacramento River. The primary factor used to differentiate the alternatives was the ability to achieve the purpose of habitat restoration while possibly reducing the potential adverse effects of the proposed action. Each alternative was screened for economic, environmental, and technical feasibility.

2.3.2 Alternative 1 – No Action

Under the no action alternative, riparian vegetation would not be restored or enhanced on the existing SRNWR lands. Conditions on these properties would remain the same, with some acreage supporting native or replanted riparian habitat and other acreage continuing with agricultural operations. There would be neither positive nor negative direct effects on the refuge lands. Without active revegetation efforts, there would be no near-term benefit to wildlife and vegetation; therefore, the objectives of the proposed action would not be met. Improvements in conditions for wildlife along the Sacramento River corridor would depend on other public or private entities. Currently, there is no other major organized and funded program to achieve the goals of the SRNWR. In the long term, other initiatives could replace the USFWS restoration program.

This alternative is inconsistent with the intent of Congress in authorizing development of an 18,000-acre refuge along the Sacramento River. It would result in substantially fewer positive impacts on the river's wildlife.

2.3.3 Alternatives Considered but Eliminated from Detailed Study

The Service did not consider alternative locations for restoration of habitat. The lands considered in this EA are already part of the SRNWR. Land has been purchased and dedicated for the enhancement of habitat conditions to benefit numerous fish and wildlife species that rely on the Sacramento River corridor for their existence. The proposed action is the restoration of habitat in these units. During the acquisition process, the Service used a number of selection criteria to identify parcels for restoration, including biological significance of each tract, existing and anticipated threats to the tract's wildlife value, and landowner's willingness to sell the property.

The Service has considered a number of alternative planting programs for the project units. To hasten the development of the habitat, the Service considered removal of existing crops as soon as parcels were purchased and funds were available to implement the planting. Although this option would hasten the establishment of habitat, it would not take advantage of the remaining productive life of the orchard crops on the parcels. The Service, seeking to minimize its impact on agricultural production in the area, has phased its land purchases and planting programs to mitigate the refuge's effect on agriculture. Alternative planting patterns and densities have also been considered. The creation of primarily dense riparian forest has been considered for all units. However, using soils information and (in some cases) hydrologic modeling, the Service is selecting planting patterns that offer the best opportunity for long-term vegetation success without risking substantial changes in local hydrology. Therefore, major expanses of dense riparian forest are not being developed on all refuge properties.

The Service has also considered the alternative of allowing passive revegetation of its refuge units. Under this action, land would be purchased and agricultural operations would cease, but tree crops would not be removed and planting of native species would not occur. Eventually, natural recruitment would be expected to modify the vegetation pattern on these properties. This alternative was not pursued because it would have no short-term value to wildlife. Also, recruitment would likely include many nonnative species with lower value to the target wildlife species.

CHAPTER 3. AFFECTED ENVIRONMENT

3.1 INTRODUCTION

This section describes the environment of the areas affected by the alternatives under consideration.

3.2 PHYSICAL ENVIRONMENT

3.2.1 Hydraulics, Geomorphology, and Water Quality

Hydraulics

The Sacramento River is the largest river in California, generating about 22 million acre-feet of annual runoff. The natural geomorphic process of erosion and deposition along the Sacramento River channel within the project area has generally been modified by humans throughout the period of recent development since about 1850. Construction of Shasta Dam (completed and operational 1944) 9 miles north of Redding resulted in a substantial reduction in winter floodflows and an increase in summer streamflows. In an effort to reclaim floodplain areas for agricultural production and protect property from floods, riparian areas have been cleared and levee and streambank stabilization and flood protection structures have been constructed. Depending on the specific location within the 76-mile project area from Red Bluff to Princeton, one or all of the local levee maintenance districts, the State Reclamation Board, the California Department of Water Resources (DWR), or the U.S. Army Corps of Engineers (Corps) may be involved in flood protection or bank stabilization activities.

Between Red Bluff (RM 240) and Ord Ferry (RM 184), the river regularly overflows its banks during storms in the winter and spring, flooding low-lying basins to the east and west (U.S. Geological Survey 1993). Four flood relief structures, approximately from RM 187 to RM 190, divert excess flow to the Butte Basin: the M&T Flood Relief Structure (FRS), Murphy Slough Plug, Goose Lake FRS, and the 3-B's overflow structure. Below Ord Ferry, the river is contained by the Corps' Sacramento River Flood Control Project (SRFCP), the majority of which was completed in the 1920s. The SRFCP is an extensive system of weirs and bypass channels that diverts enough water to the Butte Basin to prevent floodflows from overtopping the levees. The Butte Basin serves to route about one third of the excess floodwaters from the Sacramento River to the Sutter Bypass south of the project area and is valuable overwintering habitat for waterfowl. The SRFCP levee adjacent to the east bank starts at near Glenn (about RM 176). Since the construction of Shasta Dam, the peak floodflow recorded at Ord Ferry (on March 2,

1983) was 157,000 cubic feet per second (cfs). The Corps' design capacity within the project levees is 160,000 cfs. Based on U.S. Geological Survey (USGS) gage data at Colusa, about 20 miles south of the project area, the storm of January 1997 produced a higher stage (U.S. Geological Survey 1999).

Geomorphology

Bank erosion along the Sacramento River is a complex process that depends on geologic, geometric, hydrologic, and hydraulic characteristics of the channel. Fluctuating water levels, high stream velocities, turbulence, sustained high flows, debris and vegetation in the river that direct flow toward the banks, wind-generated waves, and waves from boats are all potential causes of erosion (U.S. Army Corps of Engineers 1983). Upstream of Red Bluff, the Sacramento River channel flows through bedrock geological formations that have generally contained the river in a stable channel area of the Central Valley floor. Downstream of Red Bluff, the river has exhibited more active erosion and deposition processes and has historically meandered over a wide area in a sinuous path. The concave bends of the river meanders are susceptible to erosion because of high flow velocities and turbulence. Erosion at the toe of the banks is a major source of bank failure along the Sacramento River. The Corps evaluated various sediment erosion, transport, and deposition modeling studies for the river and determined that net erosion between Red Bluff and Colusa (RM 143) was about 7.5 million tons per year and deposition on bars was about 5.5 million tons per year, resulting in a net erosion of 2 million tons per year of sediment that was transported downstream of Colusa (U.S. Army Corps of Engineers 1983).

Between Red Bluff and Chico Landing (RMs 240–194), bank protection is being implemented in the area just below Red Bluff as part of a Federal flood control project. Various public and private entities have also placed riprap along extensive reaches of the streambank to stabilize erosion-prone areas. At various locations downstream from Chico Landing, active bank stabilization activities are conducted by local landowners, the State Reclamation Board, the Corps, and DWR.

Water Quality

Water quality is primarily regulated in California by the State Water Resources Control Board and its nine affiliated regional water quality control boards (RWQCBs) under the Federal Clean Water Act, the Safe Drinking Water Act, and Porter-Cologne Water Quality Control Act. The project area lies within the jurisdiction of the Central Valley RWQCB, which establishes beneficial uses and water quality objectives for surface water and groundwater in the Water Quality Control Plan (Basin Plan) for the region (Central Valley Regional Water Quality Control Board 1998). The Sacramento River generally has excellent water quality due to its origin as snowmelt, and it supports all existing beneficial uses of the Basin Plan. These uses include domestic, agricultural, and industrial water supply; recreation; wildlife habitat; cold and warm freshwater fish habitat; and migration and spawning for salmonid fisheries. The water is generally considered soft, moderately alkaline, and low in total dissolved solids. Turbidity is generally high during peak runoff periods. The Sacramento River is listed as impaired on the U.S. Environmental Protection Agency's (EPA's) Section 303(d) list of water bodies for the pesticide diazinon, unknown toxicity, and trace metals (including mercury, cadmium, copper, and zinc). Trace metals are present primarily as a result of historical resource extraction (i.e., mining) activities in upper watershed areas.

3.2.2 Soils and Geology

The project area is within the Sacramento Valley, which constitutes the northernmost third of the Great Valley physiographic province of California—a large, northwest-trending structural trough filled with a tremendously thick layer of sediment ranging in age from Jurassic to Holocene (Bailey 1966). The refuge units exist on and incorporate several types of level, nearly level, and gently sloping alluvial landforms, including floodplains, natural levees, paleochannels, and sloughs, that are composed of sediments deposited by the Sacramento River system (Jennings and Strand 1960; Saucedo and Wagner 1992; Strand 1962). In general, the sediments that comprise the surficial portions of these landforms are of Holocene age and consist of gravel, sand, silt, and minor amounts of clay.

Overlying these Holocene alluvial deposits are the relatively young and predominantly coarse- and moderately coarse-textured soils of the Columbia, Gianella, Horst, and Laugenour series (Gowans 1967; Begg 1968; The Nature Conservancy 2001). Soils of the Columbia, Gianella, and Horst series occupy the majority of land area in the 11 refuge units and subunits. These soils typically consist of very deep, well drained sands, loamy sands, sandy loams, loams, and silt loams formed from mixed alluvium. Soils of the Laugenour series occur only in the Kohenen unit; they are texturally similar to the soils of the Columbia, Gianella, and Horst series, but differ in that they are poorly drained. Riverwash (i.e., recently deposited alluvium) also occupies substantial portions of some refuge units. Surface runoff in the project area is slow and the hazard of erosion is slight.

3.3. BIOLOGICAL ENVIRONMENT

3.3.1 Vegetation

Information about the vegetation communities at the 11 refuge units or subunits discussed in this EA was obtained from site visits, information provided by the Service (U.S. Fish and Wildlife Service 1989), and digital computer-aided design (CAD) files provided by The Nature Conservancy (TNC). Information about the special-status plants and sensitive natural communities present in the project area was obtained from the California Natural Diversity Database (CNDDB) (accessed January 17, 2001) and from the list of endangered and threatened species in the project area provided by the Service (Appendix B). Appendix C identifies the common and scientific names of plant species mentioned in this EA.

The proposed action's refuge units contain agricultural (orchard, pasture, or row crops), riparian, and restored riparian acreage, and all units contain riverfront acreage along the Sacramento River. Some units are crossed by freshwater creeks that are tributaries of the Sacramento River, and some units contain oxbows or freshwater sloughs within their boundaries.

Five natural communities occur on the refuge units: valley freshwater marsh, Great Valley mixed riparian forest, Great Valley cottonwood riparian forest, Great Valley valley oak riparian forest, and nonnative grassland. Detailed descriptions of these communities are provided in Appendix A. All these communities except vernal marsh and California annual grassland are considered sensitive natural communities. Sensitive natural communities are important because they provide substantial ecological functions, including maintaining water quality and furnishing essential habitat for wildlife. They are afforded special protection and consideration under Federal, state, and county laws and policies, and the elimination or substantial degradation of such communities would be a substantial adverse effect.

Botanical surveys of the SRNWR units included in the proposed action have not been conducted. Special-status plant species known to occur in the vicinity of the refuge units are presented in Table 3-1. Table 3-2 identifies natural community occurrence and distribution, and potential for occurrence of special-status plants among the units. Two special-status species, Colusa grass (*Neostapfia colusana*) and Ferris's milk vetch (*Astragalus tener* var. *ferrisiae*), were identified as occurring in the vicinity of the project sites on the Service's species list (Appendix C) but had no potential to occur on the refuge sites due to a lack of suitable habitat.

3.3.2 Wildlife Resources

Wildlife use of the units' row crop, fallow field, and pasture areas can be abundant during brief periods. Although the diversity of wildlife is limited, those species that do occur can be abundant. Mammals such as black-tailed hare, house mouse, California vole, California ground squirrel, and Botta pocket gopher are common in agricultural fields that are not regularly flooded or disturbed. Bird species common in agricultural areas include Brewer's blackbirds, house finch, and mourning dove. A variety of birds use row crops during harvesting and tilling. Great egret, snowy egret, ring-billed gull, and several species of raptors feed on small mammals exposed as a result of ground disturbance. Common reptiles include western fence lizard and Pacific gopher snake. Appendix C lists the common and scientific names of wildlife species mentioned in this EA.

In winter, some agricultural fields are intentionally flooded or pond water during heavy storms; these areas support several thousand shorebirds and waterfowl of many species. Large concentrations of waterfowl occupy seasonal wetlands during the winter. Abundant species include northern pintail, northern shoveler, mallard, American wigeon, green-winged teal, and white-fronted goose. Seasonal wetlands also support shorebirds, including American avocet, black-necked stilt, dowitcher, western and least sandpipers, greater yellow legs, and dunlin.

Orchards also support a limited amount of wildlife. Mourning dove, western bluebird, scrub-jay, red-shafted flicker, lazuli bunting, European starling, and house finch are known to nest in orchards. Black-tailed hare, California vole, and pocket gopher are also present in orchards.

Riparian habitat provides cover and nesting opportunities for a diverse group of wildlife species. The cattail, willows, and blackberries along the river and sloughs are used by numerous breeding birds, including song sparrow, common yellowthroat, spotted towhee, and red-winged blackbird. Several species nest in the canopy, including American goldfinch, Bullock's oriole, Nuttall's

Table 3-1. Special-Status Plant Species Known or with Potential to Occur at Sacramento River National Wildlife Refuge Units

Common and Scientific Name	Legal Status[a] Federal/State /CNPS	Geographic Distribution	Habitat Requirements	Blooming Period
Alkali milk-vetch *Astragalus tener* var. *tener*	-/-/1B	Merced, Solano, and Yolo Counties; historically more widespread	Grassy flats and vernal pool margins, on alkali soils, below 200 feet	Mar-Jun
Fox sedge *Carex vulpinoidea*	-/-/2	southeastern Klamath Ranges, northern high Cascade Range, northern Sacramento Valley. Butte, Shasta, Siskiyou, Tehama, and Trinity Counties, Arizona, Oregon	Freshwater marsh, riparian woodland, 100-3,950 feet	Jun
Silky cryptantha *Cryptantha crinita*	SC/-/1B	Shasta and Tehama Counties	Cismontane woodland, lower montane coniferous forest, riparian forest and woodland, valley and foothill grassland on gravelly streambeds	Apr-May
Dwarf downingia *Downingia pusilla*	-/-/2	California's central valley and South America	Vernal pools and mesic valley and foothill grasslands, 1,500 feet	Mar-May
Four-angled spikerush *Eleocharis quadrangulata*	-/-/2	Scattered California occurrences, Butte, Merced, Shasta, and Tehama Counties	Freshwater marsh, lake and pond margins, 100-1,650 feet	Jul-Sep
Adobe-lily *Fritillaria pluriflora*	SC/-/1B	Northern Sierra Nevada foothills, inner Coast Range foothills, Sacramento Valley. Butte, Colusa, Glenn, Lake, Napa, Plumas, Solano, Tehama, and Yolo Counties	Adobe soil, chaparral, woodland, valley and foothill grassland	Feb-Apr
Rose-mallow a.k.a. California hibiscus *Hibiscus lasiocarpus*	-/-/2	Central and southern Sacramento Valley, deltaic central valley, Butte, Contra Costa, Colusa, Glenn, Sacramento, San Joaquin, Solano, Sutter, and Yolo Counties	Wet banks, freshwater marshes, generally below 135 feet	Aug-Sep
Red Bluff dwarf rush *Juncus leiospermus* var. *leiospermus*	-/-/1B	Northern Sacramento Valley, Cascade Range foothills, Butte, Shasta, and Tehama Counties	Vernally mesic sites in chaparral, cismontane woodland, valley and foothill grassland, 110-3,320 feet	Mar-May

Table 3-1. Continued

Common and Scientific Name	Legal Status[a] Federal/State /CNPS	Geographic Distribution	Habitat Requirements	Blooming Period
Colusa grass *Neostapfia colusana*	T/E/1B	Central Valley, Colusa*, Glenn*, Merced, Solano, Stanislaus, and Yolo Counties	Adobe soils of vernal pools, generally below 650 feet	May-Sep

[a] Status explanations:

Federal

E   =   listed as endangered under the federal Endangered Species Act.

T   =   listed as threatened under the federal Endangered Species Act.

PE =   proposed for federal listing as endangered under the federal Endangered Species Act.

PT =   proposed for federal listing as threatened under the federal Endangered Species Act.

C   =   species for which USFWS has on file sufficient information on biological vulnerability and threat(s) to support issuance of a proposed rule to list.

SC =   species of concern; species for which existing information indicates it may warrant listing but for which substantial biological information to support a proposed rule is lacking.

–   =   no listing.

State

E   =   listed as endangered under the California Endangered Species Act.

T   =   listed as threatened under the California Endangered Species Act.

R   =   listed as rare under the California Native Plant Protection Act. This category is no longer used for newly listed plants, but some plants previously listed as rare retain this designation.

C   =   candidate species for listing under the California Endangered Species Act.

SSC =   species of special concern in California.

–   =   no listing.

California Native Plant Society

1A =   List 1A species: presumed extinct in California.

1B =   List 1B species: rare, threatened, or endangered in California and elsewhere.

2   =   List 2 species: rare, threatened, or endangered in California but more common elsewhere.

3   =   List 3 species: plants about which more information is needed to determine their status.

4   =   List 4 species: plants of limited distribution.

–   =   no listing.

*   =   known populations believed extirpated from that County.

?   =   population location within County uncertain.

Table 3-2. Potential Presence of Sensitive Natural Communities and Special-Status Plants at Sacramento River NWR Units

Unit:	Ryan	Ohm	Haleakala	Pine Creek	Kaiser	Phelan Island	Koehnen	Hartley Island	Stone
Natural Communities									
Valley freshwater marsh								X	
Great Valley cottonwood riparian forest				X	X	X	X	X	
Great Valley mixed riparian forest	X	X	X	X	X	X	X	X	X
Great Valley valley oak riparian forest		X				X			
Great Valley willow scrub		X						X	
Other Site Features									
Onsite tributary to Sacramento River			Oat Creek Coyote Cr.	Pine Creek		Stony Creek			
Onsite oxbows or sloughs					X	X	X	X	X
Special-Status Plant Species									
Astragalus tener var. *ferrisiae* (Ferris's milk-vetch)	none	none	none	none	none	none	none	none	none
Carex vulpinoidea (fox sedge)	moderate	moderate	moderate	moderate	moderate	moderate	moderate	moderate	moderate
Cryptantha crinita (silky cryptantha)	moderate	moderate	moderate	moderate	moderate	moderate	moderate	moderate	moderate
Downingia pusilla (dwarf downingia)	none	none	none	none	none	none	none	none	none
Eleocharis quadrangulata (four-angled spikerush)	none	low	low	low	low	low	low	low	low

Table 3-2. Continued

Unit:	Ryan	Ohm	Haleakala	Pine Creek	Kaiser	Phelan Island	Koehnen	Hartley Island	Stone
Fritillaria pluriflora (adobe lilly)	none	none	none	none	none	none	none	none	none
Hibiscus lasiocarpus (rose-mallow)	moderate	moderate	moderate	moderate	moderate	moderate	moderate	moderate	moderate
Juncus leiospermus var. *leiospermus* (red bluff dwarf rush)	none	low	none	none	none	none	none	none	none
Neostapfia colusana (Colusa grass)	none	none	none	none	none	none	none	none	none

Notes:

X = present

{ Still waiting for detailed CAD information on valley freshwater marsh, vernal marsh, Great Valley cottonwood riparian forest, and Great Valley mixed riparian forest at refuge units}

woodpecker, tree swallow, western kingbird, and scrub jay. Migratory birds also use riparian vegetation for foraging and cover while moving along their migration route. Riparian habitat near the restoration areas has been found to support extremely diverse and abundant bird communities compared to orchard, herbaceous, and early restoration habitat types (Small 1999). The thick riparian vegetation also provides cover for mammals, including striped skunk, ringtail, Audubon cottontail, western harvest mouse, Norway rat, deer mouse, and black-tailed deer. In riparian areas that retain water into the spring and summer, Pacific chorus frogs are abundant.

Several special-status wildlife species are known to occur in the general region of the restoration sites and are presented in Table 3-3 and Appendix B. However, for many of these species, suitable habitat is not present or is present in limited amounts on the sites to be restored. Special-status wildlife species known to occur on or near the restoration sites that may be adversely affected by project activities are valley elderberry longhorn beetle (VELB), giant garter snake, Swainson's hawk, bank swallow, and western yellow-billed cuckoo. Many special-status wildlife species will benefit from the proposed restoration activities.

VELB is listed as threatened under the Federal Endangered Species Act (ESA). VELB feeds and breeds on elderberry shrubs, which are legally "protected" because they are the host plant for VELB. Elderberry shrubs occur in mixed riparian forests and savannas. Elderberry shrubs are present in riparian areas near the restoration sites but are not common in the agricultural or orchard habitats.

Giant garter snake is listed as threatened under both ESA and the California Endangered Species Act (CESA). This species is found in emergent marsh habitats associated with waterways during the spring and summer, and spends most of the fall and winter hibernating in adjacent upland habitats above the water line (Hanson and Brode 1980). The species is often associated with rice fields in the Sacramento Valley. Potential habitat is present near the Stone, Packer, and Hartley Island units.

Bank swallow is listed as threatened under CESA. This species establishes nesting colonies in eroding banks along rivers and streams. Approximately 70–80% of the California population nests along the Sacramento River, mainly within the project area (U.S. Fish and Wildlife Service 1989). Nearly all of the restoration sites have bank swallow colonies, although all colonies are not active every year.

Swainson's hawk is listed as threatened under CESA. This species breeds in North America and migrates to Mexico, Central America, and South America for the winter. Swainson's hawk often nests in trees along riparian corridors or in isolated trees near suitable foraging habitat (low-growing agricultural crops and grassland vegetation). It is assumed that Swainson's hawk nests occur within 0.5 mile of each of the restoration sites. Suitable nest sites are present in or near all project areas, and suitable foraging habitat is present at the Ohm, Kaiser, Phelan Island, Sunset Ranch, and Stone units. Foraging habitat on these sites is not of high quality. Most of the habitat exists as open, disked areas or ruderal vegetation, with corn and safflower accounting for a small portion of acreage.

Other common species groups occurring on or near restoration sites in riparian areas include nesting raptors, herons, migratory birds, and waterfowl. Several heron and egret rookeries occur in isolated riparian areas along the Sacramento River; however, none are located on the restoration sites. Backwaters and sloughs associated with riparian woodlands provide nesting and rearing areas for mallards, wood ducks, cinnamon teal, and (to a more limited extent) gadwall, common merganser, and Canada goose. Nesting raptors include great horned owl, western screech owl, barn owl, red-tailed hawk, white-tailed kite, Cooper's hawk, and American kestrel.

The existing riparian vegetation and proposed areas of restored riparian vegetation do and will support several species of migratory birds. Some of these species, including yellow-billed cuckoo, require mature riparian vegetation composed of willow and cottonwood. This habitat type will support other special-status species (such as willow flycatcher) during migration and will provide nesting habitat for many other bird species.

3.3.3 Fisheries Resources

The Sacramento River provides important habitat for a diverse assemblage of fishes, including both anadromous and resident species. Anadromous fish include chinook salmon (four runs), steelhead, striped bass, American shad, green and white sturgeon, and pacific lamprey. Resident fish can be separated into warmwater game fish (such as largemouth bass, white and black crappie, channel catfish, white catfish, brown bullhead, bluegill, and green sunfish), coldwater game fish (including rainbow trout and brown trout), and nongame fish (such as Sacramento squawfish, Sacramento splittail, Sacramento sucker, and golden shiner). Appendix C identifies the common and scientific names of fish species mentioned in this EA.

Four runs of chinook salmon—fall, late fall, winter, and spring—occur in the Sacramento River. The distribution and abundance of each run is limited by the availability of suitable habitat during their respective spawning seasons. The fall-run chinook salmon is the most abundant evolutionarily significant unit (ESU), comprising about 80% of the Sacramento Basin stock (Kjelson et al. 1982). Chinook salmon support a valuable commercial and sport fishery.

Central Valley steelhead also support an important recreational fishery within the Sacramento River watershed. Chinook salmon (all four runs) and steelhead use this portion of the Sacramento River as a migratory pathway for adults and as rearing habitat for emigrating juveniles.

Historically, the seasonal flooding that covered the basins provided spawning and rearing habitat for many fish species, including Sacramento splittail and juvenile chinook salmon and steelhead. The construction of levees has caused a reduction in the overall amount of seasonal flooding and shallow water habitat in the Sacramento River system. In winter, some agricultural fields are intentionally flooded during heavy storms; these areas are used by splittail for spawning and rearing, and by chinook salmon and steelhead for rearing. Flooded areas are highly productive rearing habitats in which young fish tend to grow very rapidly (Jones & Stokes 1999).

Table 3-3. Special-Status Wildlife Species Known or with Potential to Occur at Sacramento River National Wildlife Refuge Units

Species	Status* Federal/State	California Distribution	Habitats	Potential for Occurrence
Valley elderberry longhorn beetle *Desmocerus californicus dimorphus*	T/–	Streamside habitats below 3,000 feet through the Central Valley	Riparian and oak savanna habitats with elderberry shrubs; elderberries are host plant	Elderberry shrubs present in some locations
Winter-run chinook salmon *Oncorhynchus tshawytscha*	E/E	Sacramento River	Cold, clear water with clean gravel for spawning; migrate to the ocean to feed and grow until sexually mature	High
Spring-run chinook salmon *Oncorhynchus tshawytscha*	T/T	Sacramento River; Deer, Mill, Butte, and Big Chico Creeks	Cold, clear water with clean gravel for spawning. Most spawning occurs in headwater streams; migrate to the ocean to feed and grow until sexually mature	High
Central Valley steelhead *Oncorhynchus mykiss*	T/SSC	Sacramento and San Joaquin River watershed	Cold, clear water with clean gravel for spawning. Most spawning occurs in headwater streams; migrate to the ocean to feed and grow until sexually mature	High
Sacramento splittail *Pogonychthys*	T/SSC	Sacramento and San Joaquin Rivers, Delta	Primarily low salinity shallow water; shallow, flooded vegetated habitat for spawning, rearing and foraging	High
Green sturgeon *Ascipenser*	SC/SSC	Sacramento and Klamath Rivers	Cool water with cobble, clean sand, or bedrock for spawning. Slow moving water for foraging and rearing	High
Northwestern pond turtle *Clemmys marmorata marmorata*	SC/SSC, P	From Oregon border of Del Norte and Siskiyou Counties south along coast to San Francisco Bay; inland through Sacramento Valley; on western slope of Sierra Nevada; range overlaps with that of southwestern pond turtle through the Delta and Central Valley to Tulare County	Woodlands, grasslands, and open forests; occupies ponds, marshes, rivers, streams, and irrigation canals with muddy or rocky bottoms and with watercress, cattails, water lilies, or other aquatic vegetation	High; suitable habitat in sloughs and canals
California horned lizard *Phrynosoma coronatum frontale*	SC/SSC, P	Sacramento Valley, including foothills, south to southern California; Coast Ranges south of Sonoma County; below 4,000 feet in northern California	Grasslands, brushlands, woodlands, and open coniferous forest with sandy or loose soil; requires abundant ant colonies for foraging	Not known to occur
Giant garter snake *Thamnophis gigas*	T/T	Central Valley from Fresno north to the Gridley/Sutter Buttes area; has been extirpated from areas south of Fresno	Sloughs, canals, and other small waterways where there is a prey base of small fish and amphibians; requires grassy banks and emergent vegetation for basking and areas of high ground protected from flooding during winter	Low; no suitable habitat present on sites; suitable habitat near Stone, Packer, and Hartley Island Units

Table 3-3. Continued

Species	Status* Federal/State	California Distribution	Habitats	Potential for Occurrence
American white pelican *Pelecanus erythrorhynchos*	–/SSC	Historically, nested at large lakes throughout California; only breeding colonies in the state occur at lower Klamath National Wildlife Refuge, Siskiyou County, and at Clear Lake, Modoc County; winters along the California coast from southern Sonoma County south to San Diego County, inland, occurs at the Salton Sea, inland from the San Francisco Bay through the Delta region, and in areas in Kings, Kern, Riverside, and Imperial Counties and the Sacramento Valley	Freshwater lakes with islands for breeding; inhabits river sloughs, freshwater marshes, salt ponds, and coastal bays during the rest of the year	Low, no suitable habitat present
Double-crested cormorant *Phalacrocorax auritus*	–/SSC	Winters along the entire California coast and inland over the Coast Ranges into the Central Valley from Tehama County to Fresno County, a permanent resident along the coast from Monterey County to San Diego County, along the Colorado River, Imperial, Riverside, Kern, and King Counties, and the islands off San Francisco; breeds in Siskiyou, Modoc, Lassen, Shasta, Plumas, and Mono Counties; also breeds in the San Francisco Bay Area and in Yolo and Sacramento Counties	Rocky coastlines, beaches, inland ponds, and lakes; needs open water for foraging, and nests in riparian forests or on protected islands, usually in snags	Potential roosting sites present in mature forests
Least bittern *Ixobrychus exilis*	SC/SSC	Permanent residents along the Colorado River and Salton Sea and in isolated areas in Imperial, San Diego, and Los Angeles Counties; summers at Tulare Lake and parts of Fresno, Merced, Madera, Siskiyou, and Modoc Counties; and in marshlands of Yolo, Sutter, Colusa, Glenn, and Butte Counties	Marshes and along pond edges, where tules and rushes can provide cover; nests are built low in the tules over the water	Low, no suitable habitat present
White-faced ibis *Plegadis chihi*	SC/SSC	Both resident and winter populations on the Salton Sea and in isolated areas in Imperial, San Diego, Ventura, and Fresno Counties; breeds at Honey Lake, Lassen County, at Mendota Wildlife Management Area, Fresno County, and near Woodland, Yolo County; winters in Merced County and along the Sacramento River in Colusa, Glenn, Butte, Sutter, and Yolo Counties	Prefers freshwater marshes with tules, cattails, and rushes, but may nest in trees and forage in flooded agricultural fields, especially flooded rice fields	Low, no suitable habitat present except for seasonal wetland in Pine Creek Unit
Osprey *Pandion haliaetus*	–/SSC	Nests along the north coast from Marin County to Del Norte County, east through the Klamath and Cascade Ranges, and the upper Sacramento Valley; important inland breeding populations at Shasta Lake, Eagle Lake, and Lake Almanor and small numbers elsewhere south through the Sierra Nevada; winters along the coast from San Mateo County to San Diego County	Nests in snags or cliffs or other high, protected sites near the ocean, large lakes, or rivers with abundant fish populations	High; known nests in refuge and vicinity
Golden eagle *Aquila chrysaetos*	PR/SSC, FP	Foothills and mountains throughout California; uncommon nonbreeding visitor to lowlands such as the Central Valley	Cliffs and escarpments or tall trees for nesting; annual grasslands, chaparral, and oak woodlands with plentiful medium and large-sized mammals for prey	Moderate; suitable foraging habitat present during winter

Table 3-3. Continued

Species	Status* Federal/State	California Distribution	Habitats	Potential for Occurrence
Bald eagle *Haliaeetus leucocephalus*	T/E	Nests in Siskiyou, Modoc, Trinity, Shasta, Lassen, Plumas, Butte, Tehama, Lake, and Mendocino Counties and in the Lake Tahoe Basin; reintroduced into central coast; winter range includes the rest of California, except the southeastern deserts, very high altitudes in the Sierras, and east of the Sierra Nevada south of Mono County; range expanding	In western North America, nests and roosts in coniferous forests within 1 mile of a lake, a reservoir, a stream, or the ocean	High; marginal foraging habitat present onsite but high quality habitat present near sites
White-tailed kite *Elanus leucurus*	–/FP	Lowland areas west of Sierra Nevada from head of Sacramento Valley south, including coastal valleys and foothills to western San Diego County at the Mexico border	Low foothills or valley areas with valley or live oaks, riparian areas, and marshes near open grasslands for foraging	Moderate; suitable nesting sites in riparian habitat
Northern harrier *Circus cyaneus*	–/SSC	Throughout lowland California; has been recorded in fall at high elevations	Grasslands, meadows, marshes, and seasonal and agricultural wetlands providing tall cover	High; suitable nesting and foraging habitat present
Sharp-shinned hawk *Accipiter striatus*	–/SSC	Permanent resident on the Sierra Nevada, Cascade, Klamath, and north Coast Ranges at midelevations and along the coast in Marin, San Francisco, San Mateo, Santa Cruz, and Monterey Counties; winters over the rest of the state except very high elevations	Dense canopy ponderosa pine or mixed-conifer forest and riparian habitats	Low; marginal nesting habitat in riparian areas
Cooper's hawk *Accipiter cooperii*	–/SSC	Throughout California except high altitudes in the Sierra Nevada; winters in the Central Valley, southeastern desert regions, and plains east of the Cascade Range; permanent residents occupy the rest of the state	Nests primarily in riparian forests dominated by deciduous species; also nests in densely canopied forests from digger pine-oak woodland up to ponderosa pine; forages in open woodlands	Moderate; suitable nesting habitat in riparian areas
Swainson's hawk *Buteo swainsoni*	–/T	Lower Sacramento and San Joaquin Valleys, the Klamath Basin, and Butte Valley; the state's highest nesting densities occur near Davis and Woodland, Yolo County	Nests in oaks or cottonwoods in or near riparian habitats; forages in grasslands, irrigated pastures, grain fields, and vegetable crops	High; high quality nesting habitat near restoration sites; lower quality foraging habitat present
Merlin *Falco columbarius*	–/SSC	Does not nest in California; rare but widespread winter visitor to the Central Valley and coastal areas	Forages along coastlines, open grasslands, savannas, and woodlands; often forages near	Moderate; suitable foraging habitat present
American peregrine falcon *Falco peregrinus anatum*	E/E	Permanent resident on the north and south Coast Ranges; may summer on the Cascade and Klamath Ranges south through the Sierra Nevada to Madera County; winters in the Central Valley south through the Transverse and Peninsular Ranges and the plains east of the Cascade Range	Nests and roosts on protected ledges of high cliffs, usually adjacent to lakes, rivers, or marshes that support large populations of other bird species	Moderate; suitable foraging habitat present

Table 3-3. Continued

Species	Status* Federal/State	California Distribution	Habitats	Potential for Occurrence
Prairie falcon *Falco mexicanus*	–/SSC	Found as permanent resident on the south Coast, Transverse, Peninsular, and northern Cascade Ranges, the southeastern deserts, Inyo-White Mountains, Modoc, Lassen, and Plumas Counties, and the foothills surrounding the Central Valley; winters in the Central Valley, along the coast from Santa Barbara County to San Diego County, and in Marin, Sonoma, Humboldt, Del Norte, and Inyo Counties	Cliffs or escarpments for nesting; adjacent dry, open terrain or uplands, marshes, and seasonal marshes for foraging	Moderate; suitable foraging habitat present
Greater sandhill crane *Grus canadensis tabida*	–/T	Breeds on the plains east of the Cascade Range and south to Sierra County; winters in the Central Valley, southern Imperial County, Lake Havasu National Wildlife Refuge, and the Colorado River Indian Reserve	Summers in open terrain near shallow lakes or freshwater marshes; winters in plains and valleys near bodies of fresh water	Low; marginal foraging habitat present
Mountain plover *Charadrius montanus*	C/SSC	Does not breed in California; in winter, found in the Central Valley south of Yuba County, along the coast in parts of San Luis Obispo, Santa Barbara, Ventura, and San Diego Counties; parts of Imperial, Riverside, Kern, and Los Angeles Counties	Occupies open plains or rolling hills with short grasses or very sparse vegetation; nearby bodies of water are not needed; may use newly plowed or sprouting grainfields	Low; marginal foraging habitat present
Long-billed curlew *Numenius americanus*	–/SSC	Nests in northeastern California in Modoc, Siskiyou, and Lassen Counties; winters along coast or in interior valleys west of Sierra Nevada	Nests at high-elevation grasslands adjacent to lakes or marshes during migration and in winter; frequents coastal beaches and mudflats or interior grasslands and agricultural fields	Low; marginal foraging habitat present in Pine Creek Unit
Black tern *Chlidonias niger*	SC/SSC	Spring and summer resident of the Central Valley, Salton Sea, and northeastern California where suitable emergent wetlands occur	Freshwater wetlands, lakes, ponds, moist grasslands, and agricultural fields; feeds mainly on fish and invertebrates while hovering over water	Low; no suitable habitat present
Short-eared owl *Asio flammeus*	–/SSC	Permanent resident along the coast from Del Norte County to Monterey County although very rare in summer north of San Francisco Bay, in the Sierra Nevada north of Nevada County, in the plains east of the Cascades, and in Mono County; small, isolated populations also nest in the Central Valley; winters on the coast from San Luis Obispo County to San Diego County, in the Central Valley from Tehama County to Kern County, in the eastern Sierra Nevada from Sierra County to Alpine County, on the Channel Islands, and in Imperial County	Freshwater and salt marshes, lowland meadows, and irrigated alfalfa fields; needs dense tules or tall grass for nesting and daytime roosts	Low; no suitable nesting habitat present
Long-eared owl *Asio otus*	–/SSC	Permanent resident east of the Cascade Range from Placer County north to the Oregon border, east of the Sierra Nevada from Alpine County to Inyo County, along the coast from Sonoma County to San Luis Obispo County, and eastward over the north Coast Ranges to Colusa County; winters in the Central Valley, Mojave and Sonora Deserts, and the Inyo-White Mountains; summers along the eastern rim of the Central Valley and Sierra foothills from Tehama County to Kern County	Dense riparian stands of willows, cottonwoods, live oaks, or conifers; uses adjacent open lands for foraging; nests in abandoned crow, hawk, or magpie nests	Moderate; suitable habitat present

Table 3-3. Continued

Species	Status* Federal/State	California Distribution	Habitats	Potential for Occurrence
Western burrowing owl *Athene cunicularia hypugea*	SC/SSC	Lowlands throughout California, including the Central Valley, northeastern plateau, southeastern deserts, and coastal areas; rare along south coast	Rodent burrows in sparse grassland, desert, and agricultural habitats	Low; marginal nesting and foraging habitat present
Willow flycatcher *Empidonax traillii*	SC/E	Summer range includes a narrow strip along the eastern Sierra Nevada from Shasta County to Kern County, another strip along the western Sierra Nevada from El Dorado County to Madera County; widespread in migration	Riparian areas and large, wet meadows with abundant willows for breeding; usually found in riparian habitats during migration	High; suitable foraging habitat present during migration
Purple martin *Progne subis*	–/SSC	Nests in Sacramento; uncommon or absent elsewhere in the Central Valley; breeds locally in coastal areas from Del Norte County south to Santa Barbara County, rare in southern California	Abandoned woodpecker holes in valley oak and cottonwood forests for nesting; also nests in vertical drainage holes under elevated freeways and highway bridges; open areas required for feeding	Low; suitable nesting habitat present in mature forests
Bank swallow *Riparia riparia*	–/T	The state's largest remaining breeding populations are along the Sacramento River from Tehama County to Sacramento County and along the Feather and lower American Rivers and Cache Creek, in the Owens Valley; nesting areas also include the plains east of the Cascade Range south through Lassen County, northern Siskiyou County, and small populations near the coast from San Francisco County to Monterey County	Nests in bluffs or banks, usually adjacent to water, where the soil consists of sand or sandy loam to allow digging	High; suitable nesting habitat present in eroding river banks on most restoration sites
Western yellow-billed cuckoo *Coccyzus americanus occidentalis*	–/E	Nests along the upper Sacramento, lower Feather, south fork of the Kern, Amargosa, Santa Ana, and Colorado Rivers	Wide, dense riparian forests with a thick understory of willows for nesting; sites with a dominant cottonwood overstory are preferred for foraging; may avoid valley oak riparian habitats where scrub jays are abundant	Moderate; suitable habitat present in mature riparian forest in the Phelan Island Unit
Loggerhead shrike *Lanius ludovicianus*	SC/SSC	Resident and winter visitor in lowlands and foothills throughout California; rare on coastal slope north to Mendocino County, occurring only in winter	Prefers open habitats with scattered shrubs, trees, posts, fences, utility lines, or other perches	High; suitable nesting habitat present
California yellow warbler *Dendroica petechia brewsteri*	–/SSC	Nests over all of California except the Central Valley, the Mojave Desert region, and high altitudes in the Sierra Nevada; winters along the Colorado River and in parts of Imperial and Riverside Counties; two small permanent populations in San Diego and Santa Barbara Counties	Nests in riparian areas dominated by willows, cottonwoods, sycamores, or alders or in mature chaparral; may also use oaks, conifers, and urban areas near streamcourses	High; suitable nesting habitat in riparian areas
Yellow-breasted chat *Icteria virens*	–/SSC	Uncommon migrant in California; nests in a few locations with appropriate habitat, such as Sweetwater and Weber Creeks, El Dorado County, Pit River, Shasta County, Russian River, Sonoma County; Little Lake Valley, Mendocino County, and upper Putah Creek, Yolo County	Nests in dense riparian habitats dominated by willows, alders, Oregon ash, tall weeds, blackberry vines, and grapevines	Moderate; suitable nesting habitat in riparian areas

Table 3-3. Continued

Species	Status* Federal/State	California Distribution	Habitats	Potential for Occurrence
Tricolored blackbird *Agelaius tricolor*	SC/SSC	Largely endemic to California; permanent residents in the Central Valley from Butte County to Kern County; at scattered coastal locations from Marin County south to San Diego County; breeds at scattered locations in Lake, Sonoma, and Solano Counties; rare nester in Siskiyou, Modoc, and Lassen Counties	Nests in dense colonies in emergent marsh vegetation, such as tules and cattails, or upland sites with blackberries, nettles, thistles, and grainfields; nesting habitat must be large enough to support 50 pairs; probably requires water at or near the nesting colony; requires large foraging areas, including marshes, pastures, agricultural wetlands, dairies, and feedlots, where insect prey is abundant	Low; no suitable nesting habitat
Pallid bat *Antrozous pallidus*	–/SSC	Low elevations throughout California	Rocky outcrops, cliffs, and crevices for roosting; access to open habitats required for foraging	Low; no suitable nesting structures
Pale Townsend's (=western) big-eared bat *Corynorhinus townsendii pallescens*	SC/SSC	Klamath Mountains, Cascades, Sierra Nevada, Central Valley, Transverse and Peninsular Ranges, Great Basin, and the Mojave and Sonora Deserts	Mesic habitats; gleans insects from brush or trees and feeds along habitat edges	No known occurrences
Ringtail *Bassariscus astutus*	–/FP	Little information on distribution and abundance; apparently occurs throughout the state except for the southern Central Valley and Modoc Plateau	Occurs primarily in riparian but also known from most forest and shrub habitats from lower to mid-elevations	High; suitable habitat in riparian areas

* Status explanations:

Federal

E	=	listed as endangered under the federal Endangered Species Act.
T	=	listed as threatened under the federal Endangered Species Act.
PR	=	protected under the Golden Eagle Protection Act.
C	=	species for which USFWS has on file sufficient information on biological vulnerability and threat(s) to support issuance of a proposed rule to list.
SC	=	species of concern; species for which existing information indicates it may warrant listing but for which substantial biological information to support a proposed rule is lacking.
–	=	no listing.

State

E	=	listed as endangered under the California Endangered Species Act.
T	=	listed as threatened under the California Endangered Species Act.
P	=	protected under the California Fish and Game Code.
FP	=	fully protected under the California Fish and Game Code.
SSC	=	species of special concern in California.
–	=	no listing.

Riparian habitat provides structure (through shaded riverine aquatic [SRA] habitat) and food to fish species. Shade decreases water temperatures, while low overhanging branches can provide sources of food by attracting terrestrial insects. As riparian areas mature, the vegetation sloughs off into the rivers, creating structurally complex habitat consisting of large woody debris that furnishes refugia from predators, creates higher water velocities, and provides habitat for aquatic invertebrates. For these reasons, many fish species are attracted to SRA habitat.

Several special-status fish species are known or have potential to occur in the project reaches (Table 3-3 and Appendix B). All of the special-status species will benefit from the proposed restoration activities through increased and improved riparian and SRA habitat.

Winter-run chinook is listed as endangered under both ESA and CESA. These fish typically migrate through the project area from December through July as adults, and from November through May as emigrating juveniles. The portion of the Sacramento River from Keswick Dam to Chipps Island, all waters westward from Chipps Island to the Carquinez Strait Bridge, all waters of San Pablo Bay, and all waters of San Francisco Bay north of the San Francisco –Oakland Bay Bridge have been designated as critical habitat for winter-run chinook salmon (58 FR 33212, June 16, 1993). Critical habitat includes the river water, river bottom, and adjacent riparian zone (i.e., those adjacent terrestrial areas that directly affect a freshwater aquatic ecosystem).

On March 9, 1998 (63 FR 11481), the National Marine Fisheries Service (NMFS) issued a proposed rule to list spring-run chinook salmon as endangered; however, on September 16, 1999 (64 FR 50393), NMFS listed the ESU as threatened. NMFS designated critical habitat for spring-run chinook salmon on February 16, 2000 (65 FR 7764); the designation includes all river reaches accessible to spring-run chinook in the Sacramento River and its tributaries. On February 5, 1999, the California Fish and Game Commission listed spring-run chinook as threatened under CESA. Adult spring-run migrate through the project area from March to September, while juveniles and yearlings emigrate downstream from March to June and November to April, respectively.

On September 16, 1999 (64 FR 50393), NMFS determined that fall-run and late fall–run chinook salmon did not warrant listing as threatened and downgraded them to candidate status. There is no state protection for fall-run or late fall–run chinook salmon. Adult fall-run chinook salmon enter the Sacramento system from July through December and spawn from October through December. Late fall–run chinook salmon enter the river from October to April and spawn from January to April (Vogel & Marine 1992). Newly emerged fry remain in shallow, lower velocity edgewaters, particularly where debris accumulates and helps to conceal the fish from predators (California Department of Fish and Game 1998).

NMFS listed the Central Valley steelhead ESU as threatened (downgraded from its proposed status of endangered) (63 FR 13347, March 19, 1998), and designated critical habitat for this ESU on February 16, 2000 (65 FR 7764). Designated critical habitat includes all river reaches accessible to Central Valley steelhead in the Sacramento River and its tributaries. Historical records indicate that adult steelhead enter the mainstem Sacramento River in July, reach peak abundance in the fall, and continue migrating through February or March (McEwan and Jackson

1996). Juveniles emigrate downstream to the ocean in November through May (Schaffter 1980); however, most Sacramento River steelhead emigrate in spring and early summer (Reynolds et al. 1993). Sacramento River steelhead generally migrate as 1-year-olds at a length of 6–8 inches (Barnhart 1986, Reynolds et al. 1993).

In 1999, after 4 years of candidate status, Sacramento splittail was listed as threatened under ESA (64 FR 25, March 10, 1999). Fall midwater trawl surveys indicate that juvenile splittail abundance has been highly variable from year to year, with peaks and declines coinciding with wet and dry periods, respectively, based on when flooded shallow water habitat is created. Recent data indicate that splittail occur in the Sacramento River as far upstream as Red Bluff Diversion Dam (RM 240) (Sommer et al. 1997) and that some adults spend the summer in the mainstem Sacramento River rather than return to the estuary (Baxter 1999). The distribution and extent of spawning and rearing along the mainstem Sacramento River is unknown.

Splittail spawn over flooded terrestrial or aquatic vegetation (Moyle 1976, Wang 1986) in early March and May in lower reaches of the Sacramento River (Moyle et al. 1989). Spawning has been observed to occur as early as January and to continue through July (Wang 1986). Larval splittail are commonly found in the shallow, vegetated areas where spawning occurs. Larvae eventually move into deeper open water habitats as they grow and become juveniles.

Green sturgeon occur in the lower reaches of large rivers, including the Sacramento-San Joaquin River basin, Eel, Mad, Klamath and Smith Rivers. Little is known about green sturgeon stock abundance and distribution, life history, or factors affecting abundance. The limited available information is summarized primarily from Moyle (1976) and Kohlhorst et al. (1991).

Green sturgeon spend less time in estuaries and fresh water than do white sturgeon. They make extensive ocean migrations; consequently, most recoveries of individuals tagged in San Pablo Bay have come from the ocean and from rivers and estuaries in Oregon and Washington. Juvenile fish have been collected in the Sacramento River, near Hamilton City, and in the Delta and San Francisco Bay. Adults and juveniles have been observed near Red Bluff Diversionary Dam in late winter and early spring. Juveniles inhabit the estuary until they are approximately 4–6 years old, when they migrate to the ocean (Kohlhorst et al. 1991).

The diet of adult green sturgeon seems primarily comprise bottom invertebrates and small fish (Ganssle 1966). Juveniles in the Delta feed on opossum shrimp and amphipods (Radtke 1966). Little information is available about green sturgeon age and growth; they seldom exceed 4 feet in length in the Delta (Skinner 1962, Moyle 1976).

3.4 SOCIAL AND ECONOMIC ENVIRONMENT

3.4.1 Agriculture

Agricultural Productivity

Information on agricultural production in Glenn, Butte, and Tehama Counties for 1999 is presented in Table 3-4. Countywide production values are $257,393,000 for Butte; $253,474,000 for Glenn; and $97,221,000 for Tehama (California Department of Finance 2000). Butte County's major crops include rice, almonds, prunes, and walnuts. The lands along the Sacramento River have coarser soils and support mainly tree crops. In Glenn County, the major crops are rice, almonds, prunes, alfalfa, and corn. As in Butte County, the tree crops dominate production along the banks of the Sacramento River. In Tehama County, prunes, walnuts, olives, and pasture are major crops under production. Tree crops are the predominant source of agricultural production along the river.

Agricultural Cropping Patterns

Agricultural crops grown in the Sacramento Valley vary considerably and reflect the diverse range of landforms, soil types, climate, economic factors, and cultural factors that have helped shape the agricultural character of the region. Crops grown in Tehama, Butte, and Glenn Counties include irrigated and nonirrigated pasture, rice, deciduous fruits and nuts, field and truck crops, citrus, and subtropical fruits such as kiwi (Department of Water Resources GIS data). The most abundant crops in the "inner river zone", which contains all 11 refuge units, are deciduous fruit and nut crops such as walnuts, almonds, and prunes (Department of Water Resources GIS data). Smaller parcels of pasture and field crops such as safflower, corn, and dried beans are also interspersed throughout the inner river zone. Crops grown in individual refuge units are consistent with these trends. Refuge units in the three subject counties have been and/or are used for production of walnuts, prunes, almonds and contain small sections of irrigated and nonirrigated pasture (Table 2-1).

Farmland Quality

Farmland quality refers to the ability of farmland to support various levels of crop and livestock production. The factors that affect farmland quality include physical and chemical soil properties, topography, climate, and the availability of water for irrigation. In California, two systems are used to evaluate the suitability of land areas for agricultural production: the Land Capability Classification System developed by the Soil Conservation Service (now the NRCS), and the Important Farmland Mapping system employed by the California Department of Conservation (DOC). The following sections and tables describe farmland quality in the project area according to the criteria employed by each of these systems.

NRCS Land Capability Classification System. The NRCS's Land Capability Classification system (LCC) (Soil Conservation Service 1961) is used to classify soils with regards to their general suitability for farming on the basis of soil characteristics such as drainage, water-holding capacity, erosion, and flood hazard. There are a total of eight land capability classes under this system, defined as follows:

- Class I soils have few limitations that restrict their use;

- Class II soils have some limitations that reduce the choice of plants or that require special soil conservation practices;

- Class III soils have some limitations that reduce the choice of plants or require moderate conservation practices, or both;

- Class IV soils have very severe limitations that reduce the choice of plants, require very careful management, or both;

- Class V soils have little or no erosion but have other limitations that are impractical to remove and restrict their use largely to pasture, range, woodland, and wildlife habitat;

- Class VI soils have severe limitations that make them generally unsuitable for cultivation and restrict their use largely to pasture, range, woodland, and wildlife habitat;

- Class VII soils have very severe limitations that make them unsuitable for cultivation and that restrict their use largely to grazing, woodland, or wildlife; and

- Class VIII soils and landforms have very severe limitations that preclude their use for commercial plant production and restrict their use to recreation, wildlife, water supply, or esthetic purposes.

Land capability classes II-VIII have capability subclasses that indicate the major kinds of limitations affecting land use. Land capability subclasses are indicated by adding a lower case letter to the capability class number.

Table 3-5 summarizes the land capability class statistics for soils in the project area. Approximately 47% of the project area (1,853 acres) contains class I and II soils. These soils have few to moderate limitations and are generally considered to be the best soils for the production of agricultural crops. Most of the class I and II soils in the project area are in Tehama and Butte Counties. Approximately 34% of the project area (1,303 acres) contains class III soils. Most of the class III soils in the project area are in Glenn County. These soils are severely limited by excessive wetness and physical soil conditions, but are generally suitable for cultivation. Approximately 12% of the project area (447 acres) contains class VI and VIII soils. These soils occur primarily in Tehama County and are so severely limited by excessive wetness that they are considered to be generally unsuitable for cultivation. The remaining 7% (300 acres) of the project area consists of open water and other areas that have not been assigned capability classes by the NRCS.

Table 3-4. Agricultural Production in Affected SRNWR Counties

Crop	Butte County 1999 - Baseline					
	Harvested Acres	Yield	Production	Per Unit ($)	Unit	Value ($)
ALMONDS ALL	37,207	0.61	22,696	1,650	TON	37,449,000
APPLES ALL	367	7.40	2,716	433	TON	1,176,000
BEANS DRY EDIBLE UNSPEC.	775	0.70	543	600	TON	326,000
BEANS SEED	750	0.76	567	700	TON	397,000
FIELD CROPS UNSPECIFIED	10,687					6,116,000
FRUITS & NUTS UNSPECIFIED	1,287					2,052,000
HAY ALFALFA	2,466	5.66	13,958	95	TON	1,326,000
HAY GRAIN	1,675	2.50	4,188	75	TON	314,000
KIWIFRUIT	1,307	4.52	5,908	1,140	TON	6,735,000
OLIVES	1,350	1.40	1,890	380	TON	718,000
ORANGES UNSPECIFIED	147	4.10	603	400	TON	241,000
PASTURE IRRIGATED	18,410					2,007,000
PASTURE RANGE	269,000					2,556,000
PEACHES CLINGSTONE	2,036	14.00	28,504	220	TON	6,271,000
PISTACHIOS	616	0.86	530	2,915	TON	1,545,000
PRUNES DRIED	13,675	2.31	31,589	880	TON	27,798,000
RICE MILLING	96,500	3.69	356,083	290	TON	103,265,000
RICE SEED	4,150	3.85	15,978	300	TON	4,793,000
SAFFLOWER	800	0.80	640	281	TON	180,000
SEED OTHER (NO FLOWERS)	5,874					5,000,000
VEGETABLES UNSPECIFIED	800					575,000
WALNUTS ENGLISH	18,416	1.77	32,600	812	TON	26,471,000
WHEAT ALL	2,700	2.30	6,210	87	TON	543,000

Butte County Summary:

Total Gross Production Value (All Crops - 1999)   257,393,000

Table 3-4. Continued

Crop	Harvested Acres	Yield	Production	Per Unit ($)	Unit	Value ($)
			Glenn County			
			1999 - Baseline			
ALMONDS ALL	22,562	0.49	11,073	1,676	TON	18,558,000
CITRUS UNSPECIFIED	714	6.30	4,496	287	TON	1,289,000
CORN GRAIN	15,685	5.50	86,268	85	TON	7,333,000
COTTON LINT UNSPECIFIED	598	0.59	353	1,473	TON	520,000
FIELD CROPS SEED MISC.	1,962					1,132,000
FIELD CROPS UNSPECIFIED	1,000					469,000
FRUITS & NUTS UNSPECIFIED	116					75,000
GRAPES UNSPECIFIED	835	6.81	5,683	400	TON	2,273,000
HAY ALFALFA	14,236	7.00	99,652	80	TON	7,972,000
HAY OTHER UNSPECIFIED	3,030	2.50	7,575	60	TON	454,000
OLIVES	4,490	2.31	10,357	442	TON	4,578,000
PASTURE IRRIGATED	16,270					1,952,000
PASTURE RANGE	230,000					1,610,000
PISTACHIOS	868	1.03	890	2,900	TON	2,581,000
PRUNES DRIED	8,392	1.87	15,667	939	TON	14,711,000
RICE MILLING	82,980	3.75	311,175	290	TON	90,241,000
RICE SEED	2,257	3.84	8,659	212	TON	1,836,000
SAFFLOWER	1,650	0.68	1,125	330	TON	371,000
SEED CLOVER UNSPECIFIED	2,517	0.25	618	2,754	TON	1,702,000
SEED VEG & VINECROP	3,095					3,650,000
SILAGE	2,600	28.00	72,800	20	TON	1,456,000
SORGHUM GRAIN	316	2.80	885	82	TON	73,000
SUGAR BEETS	3,110	33.50	104,190	40	TON	4,168,000
SUNFLOWER SEED	10,053	0.52	5,251	926	TON	4,861,000
VEGETABLES UNSPECIFIED	1,603					4,277,000
WALNUTS ENGLISH	7,169	1.18	8,477	775	TON	6,570,000
WHEAT ALL	15,104	2.75	41,536	89	TON	3,697,000

Glenn County Summary:

Total Gross Production Value (All Crops - 1999)   253,474,000

Table 3-4. Continued

Page 3 of 3

	Tehama County 1999 - Baseline					
Crop	Harvested Acres	Yield	Production	Per Unit ($)	Unit	Value ($)
ALMONDS ALL	6,175	0.47	2,900	1,615	TON	4,683,500
BEANS DRY EDIBLE UNSPEC.	1,200	0.88	1,050	600	TON	630,000
BEANS SEED	460	1.03	475	601	TON	285,300
CORN GRAIN	800	4.87	3,892	87	TON	338,500
FIELD CROPS SEED MISC.	253					263,400
FIELD CROPS UNSPECIFIED	1,900					263,500
FRUITS & NUTS UNSPECIFIED						3,658,000
HAY ALFALFA	4,300	6.80	29,240	85	TON	2,485,500
HAY GRAIN	4,600	2.00	9,200	60	TON	552,000
HAY OTHER UNSPECIFIED	1,000	2.00	2,000	60	TON	120,000
OLIVES	5,619	3.90	21,914	438	TON	9,598,000
PASTURE FORAGE MISC.	5,000					35,000
PASTURE IRRIGATED	22,500					2,475,000
PASTURE RANGE	930,000					6,510,000
PRUNES DRIED	10,515	1.53	16,090	900	TON	14,481,000
RICE MILLING	1,000	3.30	3,300	313	TON	1,033,000
SAFFLOWER	451	1.20	541	285	TON	154,300
SILAGE	1,000	30.00	30,000	17	TON	510,000
SUNFLOWER SEED	828	0.48	401	1,219	TON	489,000
VEGETABLES UNSPECIFIED	50					156,000
WALNUTS ENGLISH	12,477	1.32	16,470	925	TON	15,234,800
WHEAT ALL	1,500	2.00	3,000	90	TON	270,000

Tehama County Summary:

Total Gross Production Value (All Crops - 1999)   97,221,000

Source: California Department of Finance. 2001. Economic Research Website. Http://www.dof.ca.gov

Table 3-5. Summary of Land Capability Classifications for the Project Area.

	Land Capability Class and Subclass(a)							
	I	IIw	IIe	IIs	IIIw	IIIs	VIw	VIIIw
				----------------Acres----------------				
Tehama County	215	0	135	108	0	0	114	298
Butte County	0	1,228	0	0	0	34	0	0
Glenn County	10	157	0	0	1,130	139	35	0
Project Area Total	225	1,385	135	108	1,130	173	149	298

(a) Capability subclass definitions:

    w Water in or on the soil interferes with plant growth

    s   Soil is limiting because it is shallow, droughty, or stony

    e Main limitation is the risk of erosion

DOC Farmland Maps. The DOC produces two types of farmland maps as part of its Farmland Mapping and Monitoring Program (FMMP): Important Farmland Maps and Interim Farmland Maps. Important Farmland Maps are prepared for counties and agricultural regions with modern (post-1960) soil surveys, such as Glenn and Tehama Counties. They are based on information contained in the modern soil surveys and on Land Inventory and Monitoring criteria developed by NRCS. These criteria are generally expressed as definitions that characterize the land's suitability for agricultural production, physical and chemical soil properties, and actual land use patterns. Important farmland maps are generally updated every 2 years and contain eight mapping categories:

- Prime Farmland – lands with the combination of physical and chemical soil properties best able to sustain long-term production of agricultural crops. The land must be supported by developed irrigation water supply that is dependable and of adequate quality during the growing season. It also must have been used for the production of agricultural crops at some time during the 4 years before mapping data were collected.

- Farmland of Statewide Importance – lands with agricultural land use characteristics, irrigation water supplies, and physical characteristics similar to Prime Farmland but with minor shortcomings, such as greater slopes or less ability to hold and store moisture.

- Unique Farmland - lands with lesser quality soils that are used for the production of California's leading agricultural cash crops. These lands are usually irrigated but may include nonirrigated orchards or vineyards as found in some of the state's climatic zones.

- Farmland of Local Importance – lands of importance to the local agricultural economy, as determined by each county's Board of Supervisors. Definitions of farmland of local importance and potential for the counties of Tehama, Butte, and Glenn are listed below:

  □ Tehama County. All lands that are not classified as Prime Farmland, Farmland of Statewide Importance, or Unique Farmland that are cropped continuously or on a cyclic basis (irrigation is not a factor). Also, all lands that have soil mapping units listed for Prime Farmland or Farmland of Statewide Importance and that are not irrigated.

  □ Butte County. Currently has no definition for Farmland of Local Importance.

  □ Glenn County. All lands not classified as Prime Farmland, Farmland of Statewide Importance, or Unique Farmland that are cropped on a continuing or cyclic basis (irrigation is not a consideration). Also, all croppable land within Glenn County water district boundaries that does not qualify for Prime Farmland, Farmland of Statewide Importance, or Unique Farmland.

- Grazing Land – land on which the existing vegetation is suited to the grazing of livestock.

- Urban and Built-Up Land – land occupied by structures with a building density of at least 1 unit to 1.5 acres.

- Other Land – land that does not meet the criteria of any of the above categories. Examples of Other Land include wetlands, confined livestock and poultry facilities, strip mines and borrow pits, small water bodies (less than 40 acres), and rural development which has a building density of less than 1structure per 1.5 acres.

- Water – water areas with an extent of at least 40 acres.

Interim Farmland Maps are prepared for counties and agricultural regions lacking modern soil survey information, such as Butte County. Two categories of Interim Farmland–irrigated farmland and nonirrigated farmland–are mapped in lieu of the four Important Farmland categories of Prime Farmland, Farmland of Statewide Importance, Unique Farmland, and Farmland of Local Importance.

- Irrigated Farmland – cropped lands with developed irrigation water supply that is dependable and of adequate quality. Land must have been used for the production of agricultural crops at some time during the 4 years before mapping data were collected.

- Nonirrigated Farmland – lands that are used for the production of agricultural commodities on a continuing or cyclic basis without the advent of irrigation water.

Farmland statistics for the refuge areas that will be converted from agricultural land to habitat are summarized in Table 3-6. Important and Interim Farmland account for 98% (2,321 acres) of the 2,372-acre affected area. The remaining 2% is mapped as other land or water. Important and Interim Farmland present in the affected area represent approximately 0.3% of that present in the three subject counties and less than 0.1% of that present in the entire Sacramento Valley region, which consists of the three subject counties in addition to Colusa, Sacramento, Shasta, Sutter, Yolo, and Yuba Counties.

Prime Farmland in the affected area accounts for 39% of the total acreage of Important and Interim Farmland in the affected area, 0.4% of mapped Prime Farmland in the three subject counties, and less than 0.1% of the mapped Prime Farmland in the Sacramento Valley region (Table 3-6). Most (78%) of the Prime Farmland in the affected area is in the Glenn County refuge units; historically, these areas were primarily cropped with walnuts, prunes, and pasture.

3.4.2 Local Land Use Policies

The SRNWR units and subunits included in the proposed action are in Butte, Glenn, and Tehama Counties. General plan land use policies relating to the proposed action are identified below.

Butte County General Plan
The Land Use Element of the Butte County General Plan (Butte County Planning Department 1991) contains several land use policies under "Resource Management" that relate to the proposed action.

Agricultural and Crop Land

Policy b. Retain in an agricultural designation on the Land Use Map areas where location, natural conditions and water availability make lands well suited to orchard and field crop use, while considering for non-agricultural use areas where urban encroachment has made inroads into agricultural areas and where past official actions have planned areas for development.

Biological Habitat

Policy b. Prevent development and site clearance other than river bank protection of marshes and significant riparian habitats.

Policy d. Regulate development to facilitate survival of identified rare and endangered plants and animals.

Natural Areas

Policy a. Encourage the creation and expansion of natural and wilderness areas.

Glenn County General Plan

The Policy Plan, volume I of the Glenn County General Plan (QUAD Consultants 1993), contains several sections that regulate local land uses. Those that apply to the proposed action are Section 5.1.1, "Agriculture/Soils"; Section 5.3.1, "Land Use/Growth"; and Section 6.7, "Coordination with Wildlife and Land Management Agencies".

5.1.1 Agriculture/Soils

As the most extensive land use in the county, agriculture constitutes a significant component of the local economy. Agricultural land also provides valuable open space and important wildlife habitat. It is important that the County take steps to preserve its agricultural land from both economic and environmental perspectives.

. . . Converting prime agricultural land to non-agricultural uses is considered an irreversible loss of resources. . . . With the primary goal being that of preserving the county's valuable agricultural resources, a variety of preservation tools can be used. . . .

Policy NRP-1. Maintain agriculture as a primary, extensive land use, not only in recognition of the economic importance of agriculture, but also in terms of agriculture's contribution to the preservation of open space and wildlife habitat.

5.3.1 Land Use/Growth

Agriculture is the single most important component of the county's economic base, protection of agricultural land is of great importance. Land use patterns, goals and policies have been established which promote agricultural land preservation and protect these lands from urban encroachment.

. . . It is the intent of the County to promote orderly growth by directing new growth into areas where it can be accommodated and served adequately, and to avoid potential land use conflicts through the appropriate distribution and regulation of land uses. Only compatible uses will be encouraged in agricultural areas; compatible uses are defined as those uses capable of existing together without conflict or ill effect.

6.7 Coordination with Wildlife and Land Management Agencies

For all projects, with the exception of those associated with sites low in wildlife value, early consultation with wildlife agencies should occur.

Tehama County General Plan

Chapter II of the Tehama County General Plan (Tehama County 1983) makes the following statements regarding the objectives of the general plan with regard to agricultural preservation:

Preservation of Tehama County's agricultural resources was identified as a key objective in the General Plan. . . . The basic concept of the General Plan is the resolution of the inherent conflict between agricultural and non-agricultural land uses. . . . The Plan also contains other policies designed to prevent the piecemeal conversion of agricultural lands to other uses and to create a climate of public understanding in Tehama County which is supportive of agriculture.

Table 3-6. Farmland Summary for the Land to be Restored – Tehama, Butte, and Glenn Counties and the Sacramento Valley region.

FMMP Farmland Categories	Tehama County			Butte County			Glenn County			Important and Interim Farmland Totals				
	County Total (acres)	Refuge Unit Total (acres)	Percent of County Total	County Total (acres)	Refuge Unit Total (acres)	Percent of County Total	County Total (acres)	Refuge Unit Total (acres)	Percent of County Total	Subject Counties Total (acres)	Restored Area Total (acres)	Percent of Project Area Total	Percent of Three Subject County Total	Percent of Sacramento Valley Region Total (a)
Important Farmland Categories														
Prime	77,603	196	0.25	–	–	–	168,455	704	0.4	246,058	900	23	0.4	0.1
Statewide Importance	19,436	0	0.0	–	–	–	88,637	13	0.01	108,073	13	0.3	0.01	<0.1
Unique	19,492	99	0.5	–	–	–	11,075	9	0.08	30,567	108	3	0.4	<0.1
Local Importance	129,700	51	0.4	–	–	–	139,989	435	0.3	269,689	486	13	0.2	0.1
Interim Farmland Categories														
Irrigated	–	–	–	255,245	814	0.3	–	–	–	255,245	814	21	0.3	0.1
Nonirrigated	–	–	–	9,476	0	0.0	–	–	–	9,476	0	0.0	0.0	0.0
Important and Interim Farmland Totals	246,231	346	0.14	529,499	814	0.15	408,156	1,161	0.3	919,108	2,321	59	0.3	<0.1

Source: Farmland Mapping and Monitoring Program 2000.

(a) Sacramento Valley region consists of the following nine counties: Butte, Colusa, Glenn, Sacramento, Shasta, Sutter, Tehama, Yolo, and Yuba. Farmland statistics for the Sacramento Valley region are as follows: Total Important and Interim Farmland - 2,345,478 acres
Prime Farmland - 870,168 acres
Farmland of Statewide Importance - 323,293 acres
Unique Farmland - 158,856 acres
Farmland of Local Importance - 387,895 acres
Irrigated Farmland - 584,294 acres
Nonirrigated Farmland - 20,972 acres

Plan objectives focus on several land use issues relevant to the proposed action:

Agricultural Preserve Lands

Objective AG-3. Protection of agricultural lands, whenever possible, from non-agricultural development through separation by natural buffers and land use transition areas that mitigate or prevent land use conflicts.

Objective AG-4. Protection of agricultural lands from development pressures or uses which will adversely impact or hinder existing or foreseeable agricultural operations.

Wildlife Resources

Objective WR-1. Preserve environmentally sensitive and significant lands and water valuable for their plant and wildlife habitat, natural appearance and character.

Objective WR-2. Afford, to the extent feasible, adequate protection to areas identified by the California Department of Fish and Game and the California Natural Diversity Data Base as critical riparian zones.

Objective WR-3. Support and coordinate County plans with interjurisdictional programs for the proper management of riparian resources in the County.

Natural Resource Lands and Recreation

Objective NRR-1. Protection of resource lands for the continued benefit of agriculture, timber, grazing, recreation, wildlife habitat, and quality of life.

3.4.3 Fiscal Environment

The refuge properties proposed for revegetation do not constitute a significant portion of the tax base for Butte, Glenn, and Tehama Counties. When the properties were transferred to Federal ownership, they ceased to generate property tax revenues and (for lands in Williamson Act contracts) subvention payments from the state. The properties do generate a small amount of revenue for the counties in the form of possessory taxes. The amounts contributed to the counties vary annually as the cropping patterns are modified, and have represented a small fraction of 1% of the three counties' total tax revenues. In fiscal year 1997–98, Glenn County received total tax collections of $4.1 million, Tehama County received $8.5 million , and Butte County received $21.3 million (California Department of Finance 2001).

3.4.4 Regional Economy

The three-county region (Butte, Glenn, and Tehama Counties) exhibits considerable economic diversity, and each of the three counties displays an economic profile markedly distinct from the others.

Butte County, with a population in 2000 of more than 200,000 and boasting a major state university, shows the greatest diversity. The largest employment sectors are trade, services, and state/local government. Agriculture is a relatively minor sector, employing approximately 3,000 people in 2000. The value of agricultural production in 1999 was $257.4 million, ranking the county 23rd in the state.

Glenn County's population in 2000 was 27,100. State/local government is the largest employment sector and agriculture is second, employing 1,520 people in 2000. Agricultural production totaled $253.5 million in 1999, ranking the county 24th in the state.

Tehama County's population in 2000 was 56,200. Its major employment sectors are trade, services, and state/local government. Agriculture is a relatively minor employer, employing 1,440 people in 2000. Agricultural production totaled $97.2 million in 1999, ranking the county 35th in the state. (California Department of Finance 2001.)

3.4.5 Public Health

Mosquitos of the Central Valley (e.g., *Aedes* spp., *Anopheles* spp., *Culex* spp.) are vectors for diseases transmissible to humans and animals. They breed in a variety of aquatic habitats, including natural wetlands, irrigation ditches, agricultural drainage water, flooded rice fields, irrigated pastures, untilled orchards and vineyards, and waste areas containing debris that holds water (e.g., discarded automobile tires). (U.S. Fish and Wildlife Service 1992.)

The primary concern for mosquito-borne diseases in the Sacramento Valley is the encephalitis virus. Annoyance presents a non–health related problem. Mosquito abatement is required by the Public Health Code of the State of California. (U.S. Fish and Wildlife Service 1992.) The refuge units under consideration are within the jurisdiction of the Butte County, Glenn County, and Tehama County Mosquito and Vector Control Districts.

The Integrated Pest Management (IPM) program currently being implemented was developed by SRNWR, TNC, farmers and their California certified Pest Control Advisors, and the University of California Cooperative Extension IPM Advisor. This is a progressive IPM plan, with many of the practices for pest control approved and promoted by the University of California IPM program. Chemicals and biological controls are evaluated and selected by SRNWR staff in association with farming cooperators, IMP Advisor, TNC, and the Regional IPM Coordinator.

Selections of chemicals is based on their effectiveness as long-term components of a viable IPM program and the potential for approval at the regional and Washington office levels. In addition to the chemical and cultural approach, a portion of the IPM program continues to involve experiments using biological controls on deciduous orchards. IPM promotes a sustainable agricultural program able to generate funds for continued implementation of riparian habitat restoration on SRNWR lands.

Some portions of the refuge units under consideration are actively farmed, and the soils in these areas may contain pesticide and herbicide residues. Refuge management activities at some units have included the use of herbicides, as approved.

When the Service began acquiring property for the refuge, environmental site assessment level I surveys were conducted on the lands proposed for acquisition and inclusion. The surveys concluded that no known hazardous waste sites were located on those lands. (U.S. Fish and Wildlife Service 1989.)

3.4.6 Cultural Resources

Staff from the Service's Region 1 cultural resources division in Sherwood, Oregon, and the Northeast Information Center of the California Historical Information System at California State University, Chico (Information Center), were contacted to obtain information on known cultural resources in or near the project sites. Both record searches identified previously recorded cultural resources and previously conducted cultural resources investigations within a 1-mile buffer around each of the nine parcels. Additionally, standard published sources containing information on cultural resources were consulted. No field inspection was performed. The results of the Information Center records search will be forwarded to the refuge manager and by him to cultural resources division staff, where it will be available to qualified archaeologists conducting research on these parcels.

Prehistoric Context
This summary of human occupation in the vicinity of the study area is based primarily on the recent interpretation by Sundahl (1992:89–112), who identifies the initial occupation of northern California as the Borax Lake Pattern, dating from 8000 B.P. to 5000 B.P. Materially, the pattern is characterized by wide-stemmed projectile points and handstone/millingstone food processing technology. The appearance of people during this period is attributed to the migration of Hokan-speaking peoples into the region. Evidence indicates the presence of these speakers in areas north and west of the study area but not in the immediate vicinity.

The next broad pattern evident in the region is referred to by Sundahl as the Squaw Creek Pattern, which lasted from approximately 5000 B.P. to 3000 B.P. This period is identified primarily by the appearance in the archaeological record of Squaw Creek Contracting Stem points, McKee unifaces, and cobble spall tools. The Squaw Creek Pattern displays a certain amount of subregional variation. In the northern areas of the Sacramento River drainage, food processing equipment is represented by bowl and slab mortars and pestles, whereas the Deadman Complex of the southern Cascades region reflects an emphasis on handstone/millingstone technology along with projectile points of large side-notched and stemmed varieties. The Deadman Complex represents the earliest occupation of the area immediately adjacent to the project area and may reflect the movement of the Yana into the area in response to pressures brought about by the movement of the Miwok or Yokuts, or both, into central California.

The Whiskeytown Pattern (3000–1700 B.P.) follows the Squaw Creek Pattern. Sundahl characterizes this period by the presence of large and medium-sized corner-notched and side-notched points, handstones, millingstones, mortar and pestle, and notched-pebble net weights—an indication of a greater reliance on riverine resources. In the vicinity of the project area, this pattern is represented by the Kingsley Aspect, with a material culture defined by corner-notched and side-notched points along with contracting stem and leaf-shaped points. These point styles possibly indicate increased contact and interaction between groups to the north and south.

Two patterns appear after approximately 1700 B.P. and continue until the historic period: the Tehama Pattern and Augustine Pattern. Both patterns reflect the introduction of the bow and arrow as indicated by the appearance of medium-sized and small-notched Gunther Series points. The hopper mortar and pestle also appear during this period. The Tehama Pattern is represented with continued use of handstones and millingstones for food processing and the use of notched-pebble net weights, probably reflecting cultural continuity from the previous Kingsley aspect through to the ethnographic Yana material culture. On the other hand, the Redding Aspect of the Augustine Pattern tool assemblage lacks the handstone/millingstone and includes arrowshaft smoothers and bone fishing implements. The Augustine Pattern reflects the establishment of sedentary villages with a riverine-focused economy and signals the arrival of Penutian language speakers (Wintu and Nomlaki peoples) into the region.

Ethnographic Context

Three ethnographic groups have been identified as living in the project vicinity at the time of European contact. From north to south, these are the Nomlaki, Konkow (also known as the Northwestern Maidu), and Patwin. These divisions were created by anthropologists based primarily on linguistic differences. It is estimated that, when Europeans entered the Sacramento Valley, there were no more than 1,000 Nomlaki and 6,000 Patwin speakers (Shipley 1978). The Konkow have been estimated to number around 3,000 or more (Riddell 1978).

The native Americans of the project vicinity were organized into tribelets, small clusters of villages under the supervision of a headman (Goldschmidt 1978, Johnson 1978, Riddell 1978). Subsistence generally involved seasonal forays for resources away from base villages. It is reported that, among the Nomlaki and Konkow, most residents left the base villages in the summer to locations, particular to each village, in the mountains (Goldschmidt 1978, Riddell 1978). This move was driven by subsistence needs.

The native Americans of the project vicinity subsisted by taking fish (especially salmon), ungulates, small game (including rabbits and birds), insects, grass seeds and tubers, and acorns (Goldschmidt 1978, Johnson 1978, Riddell 1978). Salmon and acorns were available in large quantities. The native Americans developed technologies to turn these resources into storable foodstuffs, thereby allowing larger populations to be supported than would have been feasible with the amount of resources available in any given season (Baumhoff 1963).

In the project vicinity, the first native American contacts with Euroamericans were probably with hunters, trappers, and explorers who occasionally entered and crossed the northern Sacramento Valley during the 1820s and 1830s (Goldschmidt 1978, Johnson 1978, Riddell 1978). A malaria epidemic in 1833 killed an estimated 75% of the Sacramento Valley native Americans (Goldschmidt 1978, Johnson 1978, Riddell 1978). Many villages were completely depopulated at this time (Cook 1955). The Sacramento Valley native Americans never overcame the devastating effects of this epidemic and were unable to effectively resist the onslaught of gold miners and settlers into this region from the early 1850s through the 1880s (Goldschmidt 1978, Johnson 1978, Riddell 1978).

Historic Context

Early Euroamerican expeditions believed to have entered the Sacramento Valley between Princeton and Red Bluff include those led by Luis Arguello in 1821 and Jedediah Smith in 1828. In addition, the area was visited by trappers of the Hudson's Bay Company during 1830–1845. The Lassen Trail, blazed by Peter Lassen in 1847, enters the Sacramento Valley near Toomes Creek between Vina and Los Molinos, and provided a direct route into Northern California for overland emigrants. (Hoover et al. 1990.)

During the 1840s, much of the land bordering the northern Sacramento River was distributed in the forms of Mexican land grants. The Ryan unit is in the former La Barranca Colorada grant. The Ohm and Haleakala units are in the former Las Flores grant. The Kaiser and Phelan Island units are within the former Capay grant. The Koehnen unit is within the former Rancho de Farewell. The Pine Creek, Hartley Island, and Stone units are not located within former land grants.

The Gold Rush of the late 1840s and early 1850s brought the first great wave of settlers to California, and the Sacramento River was their highway to the northern gold fields (Hoover et al. 1990). As the booming economy ushered in by the Gold Rush began to decline in the mid-1850s, farming and ranching became predominant economic activities. By this time, valley farmers were dry farming and producing large quantities of wheat and other grains for local markets as well as for export. Dr. Hugh Glenn, in what posthumously would be named Glenn

County, became known as the "world's 'Wheat King'" (Hoover et al. 1990:95). John Bidwell, in Butte County, also raised grain, as well as planting extensive fruit orchards, manufacturing olive oil, and growing wine grapes (Hoover et al. 1990). During the 1860s, reclamation projects along the Sacramento River opened new lands for the cultivation of barley, corn, prunes, grapes, and other irrigation-based crops (Hart 1978, McGowan 1961).

Colusa County, established in 1850, was one of the state's original counties. The town of Monroeville, which was the county seat from 1851 to 1853, is described as being at the mouth of Stony Creek (formerly known as the Capay River) at the Sacramento River (Hoover et al. 1990:93). (This area is now part of Glenn County.) Monroeville could be located in the vicinity of the Phelan Island unit. William Ide, leader of the Bear Flag Revolt and an early father of the United States period of California history, died at Monroeville in 1852 of smallpox and is buried there.

Known and Suspected Cultural Resources
Information obtained from cultural resources division staff and the Information Center staff verified that the areas bordering the Sacramento River are considered sensitive for both prehistoric and historic cultural resources. Additionally, these areas may be used as traditional cultural properties. Very little of the nine parcels within the project area have been inspected for cultural resources. The cultural resources investigations that have been conducted include three narrow surveys that examined small portions of the Ohm, Haleakala, Pine Creek, and Phelan Island parcels. An additional study documents the delineation of the boundaries of CA-The-1553, but no additional area was surveyed as part of this investigation (Raymond 1991). This is the only cultural resource that has been formally recorded within the parcels. The site location is known, and the site is being protected in conformance with Federal law.

Additionally, three structures that have not been documented by a cultural resources specialist are indicated on the Nord quadrangle within the Pine Creek parcel (U.S. Geological Survey 1969). These structures were plotted as having been at this location since at least 1951 and would therefore be of historic age. Verification of whether these structures or their remains are still present at this location has not been conducted.

CHAPTER 4. ENVIRONMENTAL CONSEQUENCES AND MITIGATION MEASURES

4.1 INTRODUCTION

This chapter analyzes the environmental consequences or effects that are expected to occur from implementation of the proposed action.

4.2 EFFECTS ON THE PHYSICAL ENVIRONMENT

4.2.1 Hydraulics, Geomorphology, and Water Quality

Ayres Associates quantitatively evaluated the potential effects of converting agricultural land uses at the existing units to riparian forest using hydrologic modeling of two separate river reaches within the project area. A 2-dimensional model was used to evaluate water surface elevations during high floodflows between RM 194, south of Hamilton City, and RM 174, at Glenn. The Beehive Bend area between Glenn and Butte City (RMs 176–163) was modeled with a 1-dimensional model for the river reach within the confined levee section. Potential impacts on water quality and channel geomorphology associated with project construction, operation, and bank erosion were identified and evaluated qualitatively.

For the purposes of this EA, hydrologic modeling of alternative refuge vegetation planting plans was conducted for selected portions of the project area using a flow of 195,000 cfs, the magnitude of the flood that occurred in 1995 and for which adequate calibration data were available. The Beehive Bend model was calibrated to the peak 1998 flow 151,000 cfs but run for the design flow of 150,000 cfs.

Potential Changes in Water Surface Elevations and Inundation of Adjacent Properties
The proposed action would convert relatively open agricultural fields and orchards to more dense stands of riparian vegetation; this conversion could cause changes in the velocity of floodflows that inundate the revegetated areas. When flow velocity decreases as a result of increased friction (i.e., roughness) in the conveyance channel, the water surface elevation will rise. Potential changes in water surface elevations were evaluated in the hydrologic models described above using realistic assumptions of projected vegetation densities in the restoration areas and existing floodplain corridor at a modeled peak flow of 195,000 cfs. The resulting report shows the predicted changes in water surface elevations for reaches of the river that were modeled near

specific units proposed to be planted for the refuge. The results of both models indicate that water surface elevations upstream and within the river reaches confined by the SRFCP levees would increase minimally throughout the modeled area.

Upstream of the project levees, the results of the 2-dimensional modeling indicate that water surface elevation near the Kaiser and Phelan units would increase by a maximum of about 0.7 foot in the main channel, tapering to about 0.5 feet at the outer edge of the floodplain. The increases would generally occur upstream of the new vegetation areas due to reduced velocity and creation of a backwater effect. The 1-dimensional model of the Beehive Bend area in the segment of the river confined by SRFCP levees shows that predicted water surface elevation also rises by a maximum of about 0.5 foot in localized areas (in some areas water surface elevation is actually reduced). However, the 1-dimensional model provides an average cross-sectional value, and the specific differences in water surface elevations between the middle of the channel and the edges of the floodplain cannot be determined. Ayres Associates analyzed the existing water surface elevation during the design flood event and determined that it is substantially lower than the elevation for which the Corps designed the levees. Because the design elevation would maintain the State Reclamation Board–mandated minimum freeboard of 3 feet, the modeled project-related increases in water surface elevations would not encroach upon the freeboard area of the levees. Therefore, there would be no adverse effect from projects downstream of the upper end of the SRFCP levees as a result of the small localized increases in water surface elevation.

The duration and lateral extent of inundation caused by increased water surface elevations in areas upstream of the SRFCP levees would correspond to the frequency of flood events and the duration of peak flows, which typically are brief (i.e., less than 24 hours), during the flood event. No substantial adverse effects on properties exposed to increases in water surface elevations are anticipated because these agricultural areas are normally and routinely exposed to seasonal flooding and inundation. Local roads, agricultural buildings, and other infrastructure elements may undergo more frequent inundation. The effects of the proposed action would contribute incrementally to these existing conditions, and undue hardship from the predicted changes are unlikely. In addition, the modeled peak flow represents extreme and catastrophic flooding throughout the basin, although similar conditions have been experienced three times since 1986. For floods with more frequent recurrence intervals (e.g., 2-year, 10-year, and 25-year events) and correspondingly lower peak flows, the expected maximum rise in water surface elevation would be smaller than for the most extreme event modeled and the magnitude of impacts would be smaller. Under extreme flood conditions, project-related effects are less likely to be important in controlling the patterns of inundation than are other physical structures and hydraulic properties such as the diversion of flows into flood relief structures, backwater from major constrictions in the channel, and the location and function of the many private and flood relief project levees (which limit the extent of lateral migration of floodwaters).

No hydrologic model has been prepared for the river from upstream of Hamilton City to Red Bluff; consequently, the expected water surface elevations and inundation resulting from restoration of refuge units in that area can only be evaluated qualitatively. The effects are expected to be similar to the modeled results for the Kaiser and Phelan Island units because the modeled ranges of habitat and channel conditions in those units are representative of conditions in the Hamilton City–Red Bluff section of the river. Consequently, the potential adverse effects relating to flooding for project areas upstream of the SRFCP levees are not considered substantial.

Potential Changes in Bank Erosion, Deposition, and Other Geomorphological Properties
Erosion and deposition would not be expected to change substantially as a result of the proposed action. The predicted change in water surface elevation during flood events would be a relatively small incremental increase compared to existing conditions. Therefore, the velocity of flow in the main channel area, which is the primary factor in the amount of erosion that occurs, would not change appreciably. In addition, the conversion of adjacent properties from managed agricultural production (with associated private flood control and bank stabilization measures) to a more natural riparian condition is considered beneficial for reducing the direct and indirect adverse effects of erosion and sediment deposition in the river. A major goal of the project—planting and allowing natural revegetation of the riparian corridor—is to promote improvements that would reduce the catastrophic effects caused by the meandering of the river and associated encroachment on valuable agricultural or residential areas. The Service recognizes existing flood management and bank stabilization efforts downstream from Chico Landing and supports the need to protect the integrity of levees, weirs, and flood relief structures. The proposed action would increase the area in which the river can naturally erode and deposit, and thereby would reduce the stress on those areas that have ongoing structural flood and bank stabilization activities or that could require such measures in the future.

Potential Changes in Surface Water and Groundwater Quality
Land-disturbing construction activities for the project would be minimal because restoration efforts would primarily involve planting operations entailing minimal tillage or grading. In orchard areas where trees are removed, native vegetation would be replanted concurrently to prevent the possibility of severe erosion from disturbed, unprotected land.

The RWQCB administers the National Pollutant Discharge Elimination System (NPDES) stormwater permit program for non-agricultural general construction activities that disturb more than 5 acres. The Service does not anticipate the need to disturb more than 5 acres of ground for grading or infrastructure removal activities. In general, project construction would occur during the dry season and standard grading and erosion control practices would be followed to avoid and minimize potential discharges of contaminated runoff from the disturbed areas. In addition, if the Service later determines that project disturbances would exceed 5 acres, the authorization to conduct the work under an NPDES stormwater permit would be obtained from RWQCB.

In the future, the revegetation sites could be exposed to changes in flooding locations and inundation patterns. As a result, existing agricultural groundwater wells could be exposed to flood inundation. Infiltration of floodwater into an uncapped well could contaminate the local groundwater aquifer surrounding the well with surface contaminants carried in floodflows. To prevent groundwater contamination, the Service would periodically monitor, identify, and properly protect wells expected to be exposed to inundation, or would abandon and seal the wells according to DWR specifications.

Inundation of agricultural areas could also cause transport of pesticide or hazardous waste residues that are present as a result of historical land uses. Prior to acquisition of the refuge units, the Service conducted hazardous waste investigations that indicated a minimal likelihood of hazardous waste contamination at the project properties (U.S. Fish and Wildlife Service 1989). If hazardous materials or wastes are found during restoration activities, the Service would properly dispose of the materials at an approved facility, as indicated in the EA for the refuge acquisition (U.S. Fish and Wildlife Service 1989). The runoff of pesticides would be expected to be reduced compared to current levels because many of the existing agricultural areas experience flooding and pesticides would not be used for restoration of riparian areas. The long-term removal of agricultural lands that currently have pesticide applications is considered a beneficial effect of the proposed action.

4.2.2 Soils and Geology

Accelerated Erosion and Sedimentation

Several site preparation activities would be conducted as part of the proposed action to prepare the refuge units for planting. Some of these activities, such as orchard removal, infrastructure removal, and light land grading, would involve a significant amount of soil disturbance and may temporarily increase erosion and sedimentation rates in the project area. Because the erosion hazard in the project area is low, and because these activities would be conducted in small increments and thereby minimize the amount of land disturbance occurring at any one time, any temporary increase in erosion and sedimentation rates resulting from the project would likely be minor. Furthermore, any temporary increase in erosion and sedimentation rates resulting from site preparation activities would be offset by the substantial long-term reduction in erosion and sedimentation rates that would result from taking the refuge units out of agricultural production and restoring them to native riparian habitat.

Several of the refuge units contain riprap and earthen levees. Maintenance of these structures is not a part of the proposed action but will be a management issue addressed in the refuge's upcoming comprehensive conservation planning effort. The Service will continue to allow access to these structures for maintenance through existing easements. The Service may or may not undertake active protection, stabilization, or repairs on these structures on the basis of case-by-case examinations.

4.3 EFFECTS ON THE BIOLOGICAL ENVIRONMENT

4.3.1 Vegetation

No adverse effects on special-status plants or sensitive natural communities would occur from implementation of the proposed action. No restoration activities are proposed within existing natural areas; such activity would be limited to existing agricultural areas (orchards and pastures). No special-status plant species or sensitive natural communities are present within the agricultural areas.

Special-status plants and sensitive natural communities would benefit from implementation of the proposed action, which would increase the acreage of forest, scrub, savannah, grassland, and wetland communities throughout the SRNWR. Beneficial effects include management to promote greater species diversity, protection from adjacent land uses, and an areal increase of natural communities. Existing riparian forest, grassland, and wetland communities would be protected and their habitat area expanded. All of the special-status plant species listed in Table 3-1 would benefit from the project except Ferris's milk vetch and Colusa grass, which do not occur within the refuge units.

4.3.2 Wildlife Resources

Bank Swallow
Indirect adverse effects on bank swallow are not likely to result from the conversion of agricultural habitats to riparian forest, although some biologists believe that an eroding bank without roots makes bank swallow nests less accessible to predators (i.e., predators cannot cling to roots while depredating swallow nests). Restoration activities are not likely to increase the amount of roots in eroding banks because restored areas would be converted from orchards to riparian habitat, substituting one type of root for another.

Valley Elderberry Longhorn Beetle
Implementation of the proposed project may adversely affect VELB if restoration activities cause the mortality or reduce the fecundity of elderberry shrubs. Although the overall project will incorporate isolated shrubs in agricultural habitats or orchards into the restoration program and increase the number of elderberry shrubs in the riparian areas through planting, an occasional shrub may be affected. However, this effect would be infrequent and the amount of VELB habitat would be increased by the restoration activities. If there are instances where an elderberry shrub cannot be avoided, the SRNWR has the appropriate permits allowing "take" of up to 10 plants per year that have main stems 1 inch or more in diameter. Refuge biologists would be required to consult with the Service if individual shrubs are to be removed.

Adjacent landowners have expressed concerns that planting elderberry shrubs near their properties could lead to the spread of VELB onto their properties, with resulting special-status species issues. In response to these concerns, the Service has designed the revegetation plan for the refuge to create a 100-foot-wide corridor along the inside of the refuge perimeter. No elderberry shrubs would be planted in this corridor, thereby reducing the likelihood that VELB would colonize adjacent properties as a result of the restoration program.

Giant Garter Snake
Potential garter snake habitat will be avoided by project activities if possible. Because any project effects near such habitat would be considered adverse, the following measures will be taken to protect giant garter snake and its habitat at restoration sites where potential habitat is present near the site.

Mitigation Measure 4.3.2-1: Avoid Giant Garter Snake Habitat by Restricting Location and Timing of Project Activities. If project activities will take place within 200 feet of potential habitat between April 1 and October 1, surveys will be conducted immediately prior to ground disturbance. No ground-disturbing activities will occur within 200 feet of potential habitat from October 1 through April 1 without consulting with the Service.

Other Special-Status Wildlife Species

The proposed action will result in short-term and long-term benefits for special-status wildlife species. Most of these species (Table 3-3) have declined due to loss of riparian forest and wetland habitats; therefore, the restoration of these habitats will benefit these species. Some species may be adversely affected by restoration activities of the proposed action. In some areas, fallow fields or low-growing agricultural crops will be converted to riparian forest or wetlands under the proposed action. The conversion of these types of agricultural land to riparian forest will reduce the amount of potential foraging habitat for Swainson's hawk and other raptor species. However, fallow fields have not been providing high-quality foraging habitat. In addition, the types and quality of foraging habitat provided by fallow fields and low-growing agricultural crops are common in the region. As a result, this effect is not considered substantial and adverse.

4.3.3 Fisheries Resources

The conversion of agricultural lands to natural riparian areas will result in long-term beneficial effects on fish in the Sacramento River. This project will contribute complexity to the aquatic environment, providing cover, food, and other habitat components for fish. However, project implementation could result in temporary impacts on fish species in the project vicinity during construction. Orchard removal, infrastructure modification, grading, and placement of the irrigation system cause loosening of the soil and could result in temporary increases in sediment load to the river. Increased input of sediment has the potential to increase turbidity, possibly reducing the feeding efficiency of juvenile and adult fish. Because the Sacramento River is typically a turbid system, additional sediment input resulting from project activity would be comparatively minimal, and would not have any noticeable effect relative to the overall condition of the river. Furthermore, sediment runoff from the restoration sites would occur only during storm events.

Construction activities would involve large earthmoving equipment that could result in the introduction of various contaminants, such as fuel oils, grease, and other petroleum products, either directly from equipment or through surface runoff. Contaminants may be toxic to fish or adversely affect their respiration and feeding. With the implementation of avoidance measures, no adverse effects on fish would occur.

> **Mitigation Measure 4.3.3-1: Implement Best Management Practices to Avoid Reduction in Water Quality.** Best management practices (BMPs) could include a variety of sediment control measures such as silt fences, straw or rice bale barriers, brush

or rock filters, sediment traps, fiber rolls, or other similar linear barriers that can be placed at the edge of the project area to prevent sediment from flowing off site. The exact location and placement of the various sediment control BMPs will be determined by the individual responsible for implementing the SWPPP in accordance with changing site conditions.

The contractor will establish a spill prevention and countermeasure plan before project construction begins; this plan will include on-site handling criteria to avoid input of contaminants to the waterway. A staging, washing, and storage area will be provided away from the waterway for equipment, construction materials, fuels, lubricants, solvents, and other possible contaminants.

4.4 EFFECTS ON THE SOCIAL AND ECONOMIC ENVIRONMENT

4.4.1 Agricultural Production Effects

Farmland Conversion

Although farmland on some refuge units would remain in agricultural production for several years, implementation of the proposed action would ultimately result in the conversion of 2,321 acres of Important and Interim Farmland, including 900 acres of Prime Farmland, to nonagricultural uses (i.e., Other Land according to FMMP criteria) (Table 3-6). Because the project area would be set aside as wildlife habitat, this conversion represents a long-term loss of farmland resources.

The 2,321 acres of Important and Interim Farmland that would be converted to nonagricultural uses as a result of the proposed action accounts for less than 0.1% of the Important and Interim Farmland in the Sacramento Valley and 0.3% of that in all three subject counties. No more than 0.3% of the total acreage of Important and Interim Farmland present in any one of the three subject counties would be converted as a result of the project (Table 3-6). These percentages are relatively small when considered in the context of regional and county totals.

The conversion statistics for Prime Farmland show similar trends. The 900 acres of Prime Farmland that would be converted to nonagricultural uses as a result of the proposed action accounts for about 0.1% of Prime Farmland in the Sacramento Valley and 0.25–0.4% of that present in both Glenn and Tehama Counties (Table 3-6) (the classification of Prime Farmland under the California Department of Conservation system has not been completed in Butte County). Again, these proportions are relatively small.

The Service has taken these effects on Prime and Important Farmland into account as it has considered alternatives to the refuge restoration project. None of the feasible alternatives available would lessen or avoid these impacts. The land has already been purchased and dedicated to restoration for the benefit of wildlife. During the process of identifying appropriate land, the Service considered that the land along the river is subject to periodic inundation and therefore of lesser agricultural value than surrounding land. Willing sellers were sought so that the impact on lands with long-term value for crop production would be minimized.

Because the lands to be converted are subject to flooding, and because of the importance of these lands to the recovery of federally protected species, the Service believes that converting these agricultural lands to habitat is appropriate. More than 90% of the riparian habitat that once existed along the Sacramento River has been lost to agriculture and urban development. When the size of the acreage converted is considered in the context of the three-county agricultural base, the conversion of this flood-prone farmland to habitat does not reach the level of intensity that would result in a significant impact on the human environment.

Agricultural Production

Implementation of the proposed action will eliminate agricultural production on approximately 1,295 acres of land along the Sacramento River (this total does not include fallow agricultural land). Of this total, approximately 253 acres are in Tehama County, 306 acres in Glenn County, and 736 acres in Butte County. The crop types that are contained on these lands are indicated in Table 4-1, along with information on losses in crop production value by county. The annual loss in crop production value under this alternative is estimated to be $1,640,775, which breaks down to $998,173 in Butte County, $333,689 in Glenn County, and $308,913 in Tehama County. These values represent 0.39%, 0.13%, and 0.32% of the 1999 gross agricultural production values in Butte, Glenn, and Tehama Counties, respectively.

Based on the estimates presented above, the displacement of crop production under the proposed action would not represent a substantial loss of agricultural production value to Butte, Glenn, or Tehama Counties.

4.4.2 Local Land Use Policies

Consistency with Policies concerning Conversion of Land from Agricultural Production
As described in Sections 3.4.1 and 3.4.2, agriculture is an important facet of life in Butte, Glenn, and Tehama Counties. Multiple general plan land use policies identify preservation of agricultural land and production as important goals of the planning process in those counties. The proposed action would convert some agricultural acreage to wildlife habitat, removing it from production. The economic and environmental effects of agricultural conversion are evaluated elsewhere in this EA.

From a land use perspective, the acreage to be converted has already been purchased by the Service (i.e., the prospective change in land use was approved previously) and has remained in agriculture with the understanding that it would eventually be restored to native habitats. No additional changes are proposed as part of the restoration program.

Table 4-1. Crop Loss Resulting from Restoration at SRNWR Units

Crop	Butte County SRNWR - Converted				
	Value ($)	Converted Acres	Production Per Acre	Value ($)	Percent of County Value
ALMONDS ALL	37,449,000	238	0.61	239,547	0.64%
APPLES ALL	1,176,000		7.40	0	0.00%
BEANS DRY EDIBLE UNSPEC.	326,000		0.70	0	0.00%
BEANS SEED	397,000		0.76	0	0.00%
FIELD CROPS UNSPECIFIED	6,116,000		-	0	0.00%
FRUITS & NUTS UNSPECIFIED	2,052,000		-	0	0.00%
HAY ALFALFA	1,326,000		5.66	0	0.00%
HAY GRAIN	314,000		2.50	0	0.00%
KIWIFRUIT	6,735,000		4.52	0	0.00%
OLIVES	718,000		1.40	0	0.00%
ORANGES UNSPECIFIED	241,000		4.10	0	0.00%
PASTURE IRRIGATED	2,007,000		-	0	0.00%
PASTURE RANGE	2,556,000		-	0	0.00%
PEACHES CLINGSTONE	6,271,000		14.00	0	0.00%
PISTACHIOS	1,545,000		0.86	0	0.00%
PRUNES DRIED	27,798,000	72	2.31	146,362	0.53%
RICE MILLING	103,265,000		3.69	0	0.00%
RICE SEED	4,793,000		3.85	0	0.00%
SAFFLOWER	180,000		0.80	0	0.00%
SEED OTHER (NO FLOWERS)	5,000,000		-	0	0.00%
VEGETABLES UNSPECIFIED	575,000		-	0	0.00%
WALNUTS, ENGLISH	26,471,000	426	1.77	612,264	2.31%
WHEAT ALL	543,000		2.30	0	0.00%

Butte County Summary:

Total Loss In Production Value	$998,173
Percent Loss of Total Production Value	0.39%

Table 4-1. Continued

Page 2 of 3

Crop	Value ($)	Converted Acres	Production Per Acre	Value ($)	Percent of County Value
ALMONDS ALL	18,558,000		0.49	0	0.00%
CITRUS UNSPECIFIED	1,289,000		6.30	0	0.00%
CORN GRAIN	7,333,000		5.50	0	0.00%
COTTON LINT UNSPECIFIED	520,000		0.59	0	0.00%
FIELD CROPS SEED MISC.	1,132,000		-	0	0.00%
FIELD CROPS UNSPECIFIED	469,000		-	0	0.00%
FRUITS & NUTS UNSPECIFIED	75,000		-	0	0.00%
GRAPES UNSPECIFIED	2,273,000		6.81	0	0.00%
HAY ALFALFA	7,972,000		7.00	0	0.00%
HAY OTHER UNSPECIFIED	454,000		2.50	0	0.00%
OLIVES	4,578,000		2.31	0	0.00%
PASTURE IRRIGATED	1,952,000		-	0	0.00%
PASTURE RANGE	1,610,000		-	0	0.00%
PISTACHIOS	2,581,000		1.03	0	0.00%
PRUNES DRIED	14,711,000	64	1.87	112,380	0.76%
RICE MILLING	90,241,000		3.75	0	0.00%
RICE SEED	1,836,000		3.84	0	0.00%
SAFFLOWER	371,000		0.68	0	0.00%
SEED CLOVER UNSPECIFIED	1,702,000		0.25	0	0.00%
SEED VEG & VINECROP	3,650,000		-	0	0.00%
SILAGE	1,456,000		28.00	0	0.00%
SORGHUM GRAIN	73,000		2.80	0	0.00%
SUGAR BEETS	4,168,000		33.50	0	0.00%
SUNFLOWER SEED	4,861,000		0.52	0	0.00%
VEGETABLES UNSPECIFIED	4,277,000		-	0	0.00%
WALNUTS, ENGLISH	6,570,000	242	1.18	221,309	3.37%
WHEAT ALL	3,697,000		2.75	0	0.00%

Glenn County Summary:

Total Loss In Production Value	$333,689
Percent Loss of Total Production Value	0.13%

Table 4-1. Continued

Page 3 of 3

	Tehama County SRNWR - Converted				
Crop	Value ($)	Converted Acres	Production Per Acre	Value ($)	Percent of County Value
ALMONDS ALL	4,683,500		0.47	0	0.00%
BEANS DRY EDIBLE UNSPEC.	630,000		0.88	0	0.00%
BEANS SEED	285,300		1.03	0	0.00%
CORN GRAIN	338,500		4.87	0	0.00%
FIELD CROPS SEED MISC.	263,400		-	0	0.00%
FIELD CROPS UNSPECIFIED	263,500		-	0	0.00%
FRUITS & NUTS UNSPECIFIED	3,658,000		-	0	0.00%
HAY ALFALFA	2,485,500		6.80	0	0.00%
HAY GRAIN	552,000		2.00	0	0.00%
HAY OTHER UNSPECIFIED	120,000		2.00	0	0.00%
OLIVES	9,598,000		3.90	0	0.00%
PASTURE FORAGE MISC.	35,000		-	0	0.00%
PASTURE IRRIGATED	2,475,000		-	0	0.00%
PASTURE RANGE	6,510,000		-	0	0.00%
PRUNES DRIED	14,481,000		1.53	0	0.00%
RICE MILLING	1,033,000		3.30	0	0.00%
SAFFLOWER	154,300		1.20	0	0.00%
SILAGE	510,000		30.00	0	0.00%
SUNFLOWER SEED	489,000		0.48	0	0.00%
VEGETABLES UNSPECIFIED	156,000		-	0	0.00%
WALNUTS ENGLISH	15,234,800	253	1.32	308,913	2.03%
WHEAT ALL	270,000		2.00	0	0.00%

Tehama County Summary:

Total Loss In Production Value	$308,913
Percent Loss of Total Production Value	0.32%

Consistency with Other Land Use Policies

Along with general plan policies regarding protection for agricultural land, all three counties promote policies to protect and improve natural areas for the benefit of wildlife as described below:

- Butte County – facilitate survival of identified rare and endangered plants and animals, encourage creation and expansion of natural and wilderness areas;

- Glenn County – early consultation with wildlife agencies on all projects; and

- Tehama County – preserve environmentally sensitive plant and wildlife habitat, protect critical riparian zones, coordinate with interjurisdictional programs to manage riparian resources, protect wildlife habitat.

The proposed action is consistent with these land use policies relating to natural habitat protection.

4.4.3 Fiscal Effects on County Government

All of the properties proposed for restoration in the proposed action are owned in fee title by the Service, and, therefore, do not provide property tax revenues to county government. However, the Service does provide refuge revenue sharing payments to the counties in which these parcels are located. Several of the units do provide possessory taxes to the counties, because lands are leased for farming operations. As agricultural operations cease and the agricultural leases are terminated, the counties will loose possessory tax revenues from these lands. The lost tax revenue represents a very small fraction of the counties' annual tax revenues and would not result in a substantial fiscal effect.

4.4.4 Regional Economy

Agriculture

Implementing the restoration program on SRNWR lands would eliminate approximately 1,259 acres of producing farmland. This change in land use would eliminate approximately 27 jobs and $1,504,333 in personal income (including direct, indirect, and induced losses). These changes represent approximately 0.02% of the three-county area's total employment and personal income.

Recreation

Converting agricultural land to habitat on the refuge properties could stimulate an increase in recreational spending in Butte, Glenn, and Tehama Counties. The extent and timing of this increase would depend on how rapidly local fish and game populations increase and how access to the river properties is modified. If salmon and various bird populations begin to recover along the river, and if boating and pedestrian access to the river is increased, recreational spending in the counties could offset a portion of the regional economic losses associated with loss of farmland.

Flood Damages

The conversion of orchards and other cropland to habitat on refuge lands will reduce the periodic cost of flood damage along the Sacramento River. These costs include infrastructure maintenance and repairs, as well as other expenditures necessary to maintain current land uses. The amount of public expenditures to offset these flood-related losses would be reduced.

Summary

The effect that habitat restoration on refuge lands would have on the regional economy is a significant issue to the residents and communities along the Sacramento River. A major concern is the loss of agricultural production and resulting effects on local employment and spending patterns. Several detailed studies are now in progress for the broader Sacramento River conservation area and the riparian corridor between Red Bluff and Colusa to address this regional concern. These studies will provide valuable information to local decision makers as additional land purchases are planned to restore habitat. The loss of agricultural production on 1,295 acres that are currently under agricultural use and will be converted in implementing the SRNWR restoration plan is not expected to result in a substantial adverse effect on the local economy. The effects will be extended over a 5–10 year period, and benefits to the local economy resulting from increased recreational spending will offset a portion of the production losses. In addition, expenditures of public and private funds to repair the frequent flood damage that occurs along this stretch of the Sacramento River will decrease. The Service is funding and actively participating in the broader Sacramento River conservation area study being conducted by Chico Research Foundation (Gallo and Adams 2000). This study is focused only on Glenn County. Information developed in this study will be used by the Service as it implements its restoration program for the SRNWR.

4.4.5 Public Health and Safety

Interference with Mosquito Control Activities

Implementation of the proposed action may affect mosquito control activities in restored areas, particularly wetlands. Service policy dictates that pest control programs must be designed to maintain environmental quality and to conserve and protect the nation's wildlife resources. The control programs implemented by the Service are based on a broad, systematic approach using all available information on the life cycle of the insect, the factors that increase or decrease its capacity for damage, the nature and extent of damage that can be tolerated, and the effects of various control options on other organisms inhabiting the managed environment. An integrated pest management approach has been adopted where practicable in refuge management activities and in consideration of public health and safety. These programs are, and will continue to be, conducted in coordination with the local mosquito abatement districts. For this reason, the proposed action would not have a substantial adverse effect on mosquito control in the area.

Exposure to Pesticides and Herbicides
During the restoration process, weeds will be controlled to encourage plant growth. Weed control can occur in a number of forms, including mowing, tilling, hand removal, and chemical control. The chemical control will be in accordance with Service regulations.

Integrated pest management is the least damaging method of controlling insects at the SRNWR. However, EPA's Endangered Species Protection Program is intended to ensure that pesticide use, when necessary, does not jeopardize endangered species, and regulations promulgated under that program apply to both public and private lands.

Phase I site assessments were conducted for all properties that were purchased as part of the refuge. The assessments identified no existing contamination problems. Restoration activities would eliminate agricultural production as a possible source of contamination.

4.4.6 Cultural Resources

Damage to Previously Unidentified Cultural Resources in Unsurveyed Areas
Significant cultural resources in areas that have not been subjected to cultural resources surveys could be adversely affected by the removal of extant vegetation, replanting, and removal of historic structures (including but not limited to houses, outbuildings, and pump units). Additionally, cultural resources could also be damaged by erosional forces in places where they are currently protected by levees. This substantial adverse effect would be reduced by implementing the following mitigation measure.

> **Mitigation Measure 4.4.6-1: Conduct a Cultural Resources Investigation that Includes Pedestrian Survey and Recordation of Resources.** Before activities that could affect cultural resources occur on these parcels, a formal cultural resources inventory should be performed by qualified cultural resources specialists. This inventory should include a records search, a pedestrian survey, and an inventory report. A qualified archaeologist, in consultation with refuge staff and the Service's cultural resources division, can decide if an update to the records search performed by Jones & Stokes in January 2001 at the Northeast Information Center of the California Historical Information System at California State University, Chico, is necessary. It is recommended that the intensive pedestrian survey of areas determined by a qualified archaeologist to be sensitive for the presence of cultural resources be conducted with 15 meters or less between survey transects.
>
> Identified cultural resources must be formally documented. Consultation with the native American community will be necessary to ensure identification of traditional cultural properties. A qualified architectural historian may be needed to record and evaluate project effects on extant historic buildings and structures. The results of this inventory should be presented in a cultural resources inventory report. The report should include recommendations, developed in consultation with the State Historic Preservation Officer (SHPO), for procedures to avoid significant effects on cultural resources.

Damage to Previously Unidentified Cultural Resources during Ground-Disturbing Activities

Buried cultural resources that were not identified as a result of the cultural resources investigation could be inadvertently unearthed during ground-disturbing activities, which could result in the demolition of or substantial damage to cultural resources. This substantial adverse effect would be reduced by implementing the following mitigation measure.

Mitigation Measure 4.4.6-2: Stop Work if Buried Cultural Resources Are Inadvertently Discovered during Ground-Disturbing Activities and Assess Significance of the Resources. If buried cultural resources, such as chipped or ground stone, midden soil, or historic debris, are inadvertently discovered during ground-disturbing activities, work will stop in that area and within 100 feet of the find until a qualified archaeologist can assess the significance of the find and, if necessary, develop appropriate treatment measures in consultation with the SHPO and other appropriate agencies.

Damage to Previously Unidentified Human Remains

Human remains that were not identified as a result of a cultural resources investigation could be inadvertently unearthed during ground-disturbing activities, which could result in the demolition or substantial damage to those remains. This substantial adverse effect would be reduced by implementing the following mitigation measure.

Mitigation Measure 4.4.6-3: Comply with Federal Laws Pertaining to the Discovery of Human Remains. If human remains are discovered during project activities, the county coroner or sheriff should be called to determine if the remains are of native American origin. When human remains are discovered on federal land and determined to be of native American origin, the responsible federal agency is required to comply with requirements of the Native American Graves Protection and Repatriation Act (NAGPRA) (see Chapter 5). The regulations implementing the requirements of NAGPRA relating to the inadvertent discovery of human remains of native American origin are described in 43 CFR, Part 10, Subpart B, Section 10.4. and include the following provisions which should be implemented by the Service:

■ cease activity in the area of discovery and protect the human remains;

■ take steps to secure and protect the human remains;

■ notify the Indian tribe or tribes likely to be culturally affiliated with the discovered human remains within 1 working day; and

■ initiate consultation with the Indian tribe or tribes in accordance with regulations described in 43 CFR, Part 10, Subpart B, Section 10.5.

4.5 CUMULATIVE EFFECTS

Cumulative effects are the environmental impacts resulting from the incremental effects of a proposed action when added to other past, present, and reasonably foreseeable future actions, both Federal and nonfederal. Cumulative effects can result from individually minor but collectively substantial actions taking place over a period of time. The restoration of riparian habitat within the SRNWR units and subunits would represent a cumulative benefit to the long-term conservation of endangered and threatened species and biological diversity in the region. The restoration of habitat may, however, restrict the potential future conversion of lands within the Sacramento Valley to other uses. Cumulative impacts on wildlife, special-status species, and unique biological communities would be beneficial.

The conversion of 2,321 acres of Important and Interim Farmland, including 900 acres of prime farmland, would contribute towards the incremental, cumulative conversion of these land resources in Glenn, Butte, and Tehama Counties as well as in the Sacramento Valley and the state of California as a whole. The cumulative economic effect of this conversion could be offset by conditions described below.

The loss of jobs and income resulting from farmland conversion would be an indirect adverse effect on fiscal resources in the Sacramento Valley and the three subject counties. This effect would be most pronounced following the initial 5- to 10-year period of conversion and restoration. In the long term, the lost economic benefits of agricultural production could be replaced in part by increased recreation-based income resulting from visitor use of the river and surrounding riparian habitat. In addition, cost savings associated with the reduced extent of flood damage repairs in these counties would offset some of the economic loss. The net effect is not expected to be substantial.

The restoration would not result in substantial hydraulic or hydrologic effects on the Sacramento River.

4.6 UNAVOIDABLE ADVERSE EFFECTS

Farmland conversion resulting from the proposed action would be a direct adverse effect on farmland resources in the Sacramento Valley and the three subject counties. This effect is not deemed to have a significant impact on the human environment.

4.7 SHORT-TERM USES VERSUS LONG-TERM PRODUCTIVITY

The refuge units and subunits considered for restoration under the proposed action are part of the SRNWR. As such, the land has been set aside to serve the purposes of the National Wildlife Refuge System—that is, to benefit wildlife species in the Sacramento Valley.

The local short-term uses of the environment under the proposed action would be restoration and enhancement of riparian habitat along the Sacramento River and in the refuge units. This action would involve the loss of agricultural productivity in these units. The long-term productivity resulting from the proposed action would include increased protection and management of threatened and endangered species, wintering waterfowl, nesting and migrating shorebirds, and many wetland- and water-dependent species. The public could also gain long-term opportunities for wildlife-oriented education and enhanced quality of life.

Maintenance of flood conveyance capacity and bank protection programs along the Sacramento River would be unaffected. As described in Section 4.2, the Service's short-term habitat restoration and long-term management plans would be developed to ensure that the flood conveyance capacity of the river is maintained.

4.8 IRREVERSIBLE AND IRRETRIEVABLE COMMITMENT OF RESOURCES

There would be no irreversible and irretrievable commitment of resources associated with restoration of lands in the 11 SRNWR units and subunits. Conversion of agricultural land to habitat would require removal of crops and farming infrastructure, but this is not irreversible.

CHAPTER 5. COORDINATION, CONSULTATION, AND COMPLIANCE

5.1 AGENCY COORDINATION

During preparation of this EA, the Service met with representatives of the Sacramento River Conservation Area (a nonprofit organization) and its technical advisory committee. Agencies, groups, and individuals interested in the proposed action are encouraged to review the document during the 45-day public review and comment period, as specified in the cover letter associated with this document. The EA is also available for review on the Service's website at http://pacific.fws.gov/planning.

5.2 ENVIRONMENTAL REVIEW AND CONSULTATION

5.2.1 National Environmental Policy Act

As a Federal agency, the Service must comply with provisions of NEPA. An EA is required under NEPA to evaluate reasonable alternatives that will meet the stated objectives, and to assess the significance of possible environmental, social, and economic effects on the human environment. The EA serves as the basis for determining whether implementation of the proposal would constitute a major Federal action significantly affecting the quality of the human environment. The EA facilitates the inclusion of government agencies and the public in the decision-making process.

5.2.2 Farmland Protection Policy Act

The Farmland Protection Policy Act requires Federal agencies to

- identify the quantity of farmland "actually converted" by Federal programs;

- identify and take into account the adverse effects of Federal programs on the preservation of farmland;

- consider alternative actions, as appropriate, that could reduce such adverse effects; and

- ensure that such Federal programs, to the extent practicable, are compatible with state, local, and private programs and policies to protect farmland.

Chapter 3 of this EA identifies the quantity of farmland that is within the project area, and Chapter 4 identifies the amount of farmland that may be converted to nonfarming uses under each alternative. The Service will also send a copy of this EA to NRCS for its review with regard to farmland conversion.

In compliance with the Farmland Protection Policy Act, the Service has identified and taken into account possible adverse effects on farmland and has considered alternative actions that could reduce such adverse effects. Results of the Service's analysis of farmland displacement are provided in Chapter 4 of this EA.

5.2.3 National Historic Preservation Act and Other Cultural Resources Regulations

National Historic Preservation Act
Under 40 CFR, Part 1502.25(a) of NEPA, federal agencies are directed to comply with the National Historic Preservation Act (NHPA). Two sections of the NHPA, Section 110 and Section 106, are relevant to this project.

Section 110 of the NHPA requires that "the heads of all federal agencies shall assume responsibility for the preservation of historic properties which are owned or controlled by such agency" (Section 110 [a][1]). To accomplish this task, the federal agency should identify the historic properties within its jurisdiction and consider how the properties will be affected by proposed activities.

Federal agencies that permit, fund, or approve a project must comply with Section 106 of the NHPA. Section 106 requires that, before beginning any undertaking, a federal agency must take into account the effects of the undertaking on historic properties and afford the Office of Historic Preservation (OHP) an opportunity to comment on these actions. Specific regulations regarding compliance with Section 106 state that, although the tasks necessary to comply with Section 106 may be delegated to others, the federal agency is ultimately responsible for ensuring that the Section 106 process is completed according to federal regulations (36 CFR, Part 800.2[a][3]). The federal agency is also responsible to ensure that Indian tribes are invited to participate in the Section 106 process (36 CFR, Part 800.3[f]). Tribal representatives may be able to identify sites of "religious and cultural significance to them"—known as traditional cultural properties—that are located off of tribal lands (36 CFR, Part 800[a][4]).

Executive Order 13007
Executive Order 13007 was issued in 1996 to protect native American religious practices and sites. This order states that native American religious practitioners will be accommodated access to sacred sites on Federal lands. Additionally, avoidance of "adversely affecting the physical integrity of such sacred sites" is the responsibility of "each executive branch agency".

Native American Graves Protection and Repatriation Act
NAGPRA specifies the procedures that agencies must follow when burials of native American origin are found on Federal land (43 CFR, Part 10). If human remains of native American origin are discovered on Federal land, it is necessary to comply with NAGPRA regulations pertaining to discovery of human remains of native American origin on Federal land.

Service Compliance
The Service has completed a search of the California Historical Resources Information System to identify historic and prehistoric sites within the project area. A copy of this EA has been provided to the SHPO for review and comment. Section 106 compliance will be conducted as described in the Service's EA on refuge purchase (U.S. Fish and Wildlife Service 1989). This compliance will take place when specific planting plans have been developed and will be completed before planting commences. The Service will be required to complete additional compliance under the NHPA and other cultural resource preservation laws for any restoration and management actions.

5.2.4 Endangered Species Act

Refuge staff will initiate intra-Service Section 7 consultation with the Service's Endangered Species Division as required under the requirements of the ESA for restoration activities at 11 units and subunits of the SRNWR

The Service will also contact NMFS regarding potential impacts on federally protected anadromous fish species and will provide a copy of this EA for review.

5.2.5 Other Federal Laws, Regulations, and Executive Orders

In undertaking the proposed action, the Service would comply with the following Federal laws, executive orders, and legislative acts:

- Executive Order 11988, Floodplain Management

- Executive Order 12372, Intergovernmental Review of Federal Programs

- Executive Order 11593, Protection of Historical, Archaeological, and Scientific Properties

- Executive Order 11990, Protection of Wetlands

- Executive Order 12996, Management and General Public Use of the National Wildlife Refuge System

- Executive Order 12898, Departmental Policy on Environmental Justice

- Secretarial Order 3127, Hazardous Substances Determinations

- Refuge Recreation Act, as amended

- Refuge System Administration Act, as amended

- National Wildlife Refuge Improvement Act

5.2.6 Distribution and Availability

Copies of this EA have been sent to Federal and state legislative delegations, agencies, county and city governments, landowners, private groups, and interested individuals (see Appendix D for distribution list). Copies of the draft and final documents will also be mailed to local libraries throughout the region and will be made available to anyone who may wish to review them. Additional copies of this document are available from:

U.S. Fish and Wildlife Service
Sacramento National Wildlife Refuge Complex
752 County Road 99W
Willows, CA 95988
Telephone: 530/934-2801

This EA is also available on the Service's website at http://pacific.fws.gov/planning.

5.3 LIST OF PREPARERS

Chris Brown, Computer-aided design (CAD) analyst, Jones & Stokes, Sacramento, California
Alison Fisher, botanist, Jones & Stokes, Sacramento, California
Scott Frazier, soil scientist, Jones & Stokes, Sacramento, California
Larry Goral, technical editor, Jones & Stokes, Sacramento, California
Jeff Lafer, hydrologist and water quality scientist, Jones & Stokes, Sacramento, California
Debra Lilly, project coordinator/environmental planner, Jones & Stokes, Sacramento, California
Gregg Roy, economist, Jones & Stokes, Sacramento, California
Mike Rushton, principal-in-charge, Jones & Stokes, Sacramento, California
Tony Rypich, graphic artist, Jones & Stokes, Sacramento, California
Karen Shaffer, project manager, Jones & Stokes, Sacramento, California
Todd Sloat, wildlife biologist, Jones & Stokes, Sacramento, California
Thomas W. Smith, P.E., G.E., water resources/geotechnical engineer, Ayres Associates, Sacramento, California
Stephanie Theis, fisheries biologist, Jones & Stokes, Sacramento, California

5.4 REFERENCES

5.3.3 Printed References

Bailey, E. H. 1966. Geology of northern California. Bulletin 190. California Division of Mines and Geology. Sacramento, CA.

Barnhart, R. A. 1986. Species profiles: life histories and environmental requirements of coastal fishes and invertebrates (Pacific Southwest) - steelhead. (Biological Report 82[11.60], TR EL-82-4.) Prepared for U.S. Fish and Wildlife Service, Washington, DC, and the U.S. Army Corps of Engineers, Vicksburg, MS.

Baumhoff, M. A. 1963. Ecological determinants of aboriginal California populations. University of California Publications in American Archaeology and Ethnology 49(2):155-236.

Baxter, R. D. 1999. Status of splittail in California. California Fish and Game 85(1):28-30.

Begg, E. L. 1968. Soil survey of Glenn County, California. USDA Soil Conservation Service in cooperation with the University of California Agricultural Experiment Station. U.S. Government Printing Office. Washington, DC.

Butte County Planning Department. 1991. Land use element, Butte County general plan. Oroville, CA.

California Department of Finance. 2001. Economic research website. http://www.dof.ca.gov.

California Department of Fish and Game. 1998. A status review of the spring-run chinook salmon (Oncorhynchus tshawytscha) in the Sacramento River drainage. Fish and Game Commission. Sacramento, CA.

California Natural Diversity Database. 2000. Computer database search of the U.S. Geological Survey 7.5-minute maps for Red Bluff East, Los Molinos, Ord Ferry, Llano Seco, Princeton, & Butte City quadrangles. California Department of Fish and Game, Sacramento, CA. Accessed 1/17/01.

Central Valley Regional Water Quality Control Board. 1998. Water quality control plan, Central Valley region, Sacramento River and San Joaquin River basins. Sacramento, CA.

Cook, S. F. 1955. The epidemic of 1830–1833 in California and Oregon. University of California Anthropological Records 16(3):303-326.

Department of Water Resources. GIS data. Statewide Planning Branch, Division of Planning and Local Assistance, Sacramento, CA. Additional data retrieved from http://www.waterplan.water.ca.gov/landwateruse/landuse/ludataindex.htm.

Gallo, R. G., and D. E. Adams. 2000. The economic impact on Glenn County of public land acquisition and habitat restoration activities in the Sacramento River conservation area. December. U.S. Fish and Wildlife Service Contract Number 11332-9-G018. With assistance from Bridget Caputo, Chico Research Foundation, Office of Sponsored Programs, California State University, Chico, CA.

Ganssle, D. 1966. Fishes and decapods of San Pablo and Suisun Bay. In: D. W. Kelley (ed.), Ecological studies of the Sacramento–San Joaquin Estuary, Part 1. Game Fish Bulletin 133. California Department of Fish and Game. Sacramento, CA.

Goldschmidt, W. 1978. Nomlaki. Pages 341–349 in R. F. Heizer (ed.), Handbook of North American Indians. Volume 8: California. Smithsonian Institution. Washington, DC.

Gowans, K. D. 1967. Soil survey: Tehama Valley, California. USDA Soil Conservation Service. U.S. Government Printing Offoce. Washington, DC.

Hansen, C., and J. Brode. 1980. Status of the giant garter snake (*Thamnophis couchi gigas*). Inland Fisheries Endangered Species Program. Special Publication 80-5. Sacramento, CA.

Hart, J. D. 1978. A companion to California. Oxford University Press, New York.

Holland, R. F. 1986. Preliminary descriptions of the terrestrial natural communities of California. State of California, The Resources Agency, Department of Fish and Game Publication. Sacramento, CA.

Hoover, M. B., H. E. Rensch, and E. G. Rensch. 1990. Historic spots in California. Revised and updated by D. Okyle. 3rd edition. Stanford University Press. Stanford, CA.

Jennings, C. W. and R. G. Strand. 1960. Geologic Map of California, Ukiah sheet. O. P. Jenkins Edition. Third Printing. Scale 1:250,000. California Division of Mines and Geology. Sacramento, CA.

Johnson, P. 1978. Patwin. Pages 350–360 in R. F. Heizer (ed.), Handbook of North American Indians. Volume 8: California. Smithsonian Institution. Washington, DC.

Jones & Stokes. 1999. Use of floodplain habitat of the Sacramento and American Rivers by juvenile chinook salmon and other fish species. Prepared for Sacramento Area Flood Control Agency. Sacramento, CA.

Kjelson, M. J., P. F. Raquel, and F. W. Fisher. 1982. Life history of fall run chinook salmon (*Oncorhynchus tshawytscha*) in the Sacramento-San Joaquin Estuary, California. In: Estuarine Comparisons, edition 7. U. S. Kennedy (editor), Academic Press, New York. Pp. 393-411.

Kohlhorst, D. W., L. W. Botsford, J. S. Brennan, and G. M. Cailliet. 1991. Aspects of the structure and dynamics of an exploited central California population of white sturgeon (*Acipenser transmontanus*). In: P., Williot (ed.), Acipenser: acts of the first international sturgeon symposium. October 3–6, 1989. Bordeaux, France, Cemagref-Dicova. Pp. 277–293.

McEwan, D., and T. A. Jackson. 1996. Steelhead restoration and management plan for California. California Department of Fish and Game, Inland Fisheries Division. Sacramento, CA.

McGowan, J. A. 1961. History of the Sacramento Valley. Lewis Hill Publishing Co., New York.

Moyle, P. B. 1976. Inland fishes of California. University of California Press. Berkeley, CA.

Moyle, P. B., J. E. Williams, and E. D. Wikramanayoke. 1989. Fish species of special concern of California. California Department of Fish and Game. Rancho Cordova, CA.

QUAD Consultants. 1993. Policy plan, Glenn County general plan, Volume I. June. Fresno, CA. Prepared for Glenn County Board of Supervisors, Willows, CA.

Radtke, L. D. 1966. Distribution of smelt, juvenile sturgeon and starry flounder in the Sacramento–San Joaquin Delta. In S. L. Turner and D. W. Kelley (eds), Ecological studies of the Sacramento–San Joaquin Delta, Part II. Game Fish Bulletin 136. California Department of Fish and Game. Sacramento, CA. pp. 115–119.

Raymond, A. 1991. Cultural resource survey at the Ohm mounds site Sacramento River National Wildlife Refuge Tehama County, California. Prepared by and for the U.S. Fish and Wildlife Service. Portland, OR.

Reynolds, F. L., T. Mills, R. Benthin, and A. Low. 1993. Central Valley anadromous fisheries and associated riparian and wetlands areas protection and restoration action plan. Draft. California Department of Fish and Game, Inland Fisheries Division. Sacramento, CA.

Riddell, F. 1978. Maidu and Konkow. Pages 370–386 in R. F. Heizer (ed.), Handbook of North American Indians. Volume 8: California. Smithsonian Institution. Washington, DC.

Saucedo, G. J. and D. L. Wagner. 1992. Geologic map of the Chico quadrangle, California, 1:250,000. California Division of Mines and Geology. Sacramento, CA.

Schaffter, R. G. 1980. Fish occurrence, size, and distribution in the Sacramento River near Hood, California, during 1973 and 1974. (Administrative Report No. 80-3.) California Department of Fish and Game. Sacramento, CA.

Shipley, W. F. 1978. Native languages of California. Pages 80–90 in R. F. Heizer (ed.), Handbook of North American Indians. Volume 8: California. Smithsonian Institution. Washington, DC.

Skinner, J. E. 1962. An historical view of the fish and wildlife resources of the San Francisco Bay Area. Game Water Projects Branch Report No. 1. California Department of Fish and Game. Sacramento, CA.

Small, S., J. DeStaebler, G. R. Geupel, and A. King. 1999. Landbird response to riparian restoration on the Sacramento River system: preliminary results of the 1997 and 1998 field season. Submitted to The Nature Conservancy and U.S. Fish and Wildlife Service, October 1999, by Point Reyes Bird Observatory, Stinson Beach, CA.

Sommer, T., R. Baxter, and B. Herbold. 1997. Resilience of splittail in the Sacramento-San Joaquin Estuary. Transactions of the American Fisheries Society 126:961-976.

Strand, R. G. 1962. Geologic map of California, Redding sheet. O. P. Jenkins Edition. Fourth Printing. Scale 1:250,000. California Division of Mines and Geology. Sacramento, CA.

Sundahl, E. 1992. Cultural patterns and chronology in the northern Sacramento River drainage. Pages 89–112 in M. D. Rosen, L. E. Christenson, and D. Laylander (eds.), Proceedings of the Society for California Archaeology 5. Society for California Archaeology. San Diego, CA.

Tehama County. 1983. Tehama County general plan. March 1, 1983. Resources Group and Community Development Group. Red Bluff, CA.

The Nature Conservacy. 2001. Modern soil survey information for Butte County. Chico, CA.

U.S. Army Corps of Engineers. 1983. Sacramento River and tributaries bank protection and erosion control investigation, California. Sediment Transport Studies. Sacramento District. Sacramento, CA.

U.S. Fish and Wildlife Service. 1989. Environmental assessment—proposed Sacramento River National Wildlife Refuge—Colusa, Glenn, Butte, and Tehama Counties, California. March. Portland, OR.

_____. 1992. Environmental assessment—proposed management plan for the Llano Seco Unit of the Sacramento River National Wildlife Refuge, Butte and Glenn Counties, California. June. Willows, CA.

U.S. Geological Survey. 1951 (photorevised in 1969). 7.5-minute series (topographic) maps for the Nord, California quadrangle. Denver, CO.

_____. 1994. Flood data for the Sacramento River and Butte basin, Sacramento Valley, California 1980–1990. Open-file Report 93-68. Sacramento, CA.

_____. 1999. Water resources data – California, water year 1999, Volume 4 – northern Central Valley basins and the Great Basin from Honey Lake basin to the Oregon State Line.

U.S. Soil Conservation Service. 1961. Land-capability classification. Agricultural Handbook No. 210. U.S. Department of Agriculture. Washington, DC.

Vogel, D. A., and K. R. Marine. 1992. An assessment of the appraisal study of options for improving fish passage at Red Bluff Diversion Dam. Red Bluff, CA.

Wang, J. C. S. 1986. Fishes of the Sacramento-San Joaquin estuary and adjacent waters, California: a guide to the early life histories. (FS/10-4ATR86-9.) California Department of Water Resources. Sacramento, CA. Prepared for Interagency Ecological Study Program for the Sacramento-San Joaquin Estuary, Sacramento, CA.

5.3.4 Personal Communications

Vega, Ramon. Refuge manager. Sacramento River National Wildlife Refuge, U.S. Fish and Wildlife Service, Willows, CA. January 25, 2001 – telephone conversation.

APPENDIX A. HOLLAND
CLASSIFICATIONS (1986)

APPENDIX A. HOLLAND CLASSIFICATIONS (1986)

The following classifications are taken from Preliminary Descriptions of the Terrestrial Natural Communities of California (R. F. Holland. 1986. State of California, The Resources Agency, California Department of Fish and Game Publication. Sacramento, CA).

FOREST, SCRUB, AND SAVANNA CLASSIFICATIONS

Great Valley Cottonwood Riparian Forest (61410)

A dense, broadleafed, winter-deciduous riparian forest dominated by *Populus fremontii* and *Salix goodingii*. Understories are dense, with abundant vegetative reproduction of canopy dominants. *Vitis californica* is the most conspicuous liana. Scattered seedlings and saplings of shade-tolerant species such as *Acer negundo* var. *californica* or *Fraxinus latifolia* may be found, but frequent flooding prevents their reaching into the canopy. SITE FACTORS: Fine-grained alluvial soils near perennial or nearly-perennial streams that provide subsurface irrigation even when the channel is dry. These sites are inundated yearly during spring, resulting in annual input of nutrients, soil, and new germination sites. Intergrades at sites higher and farther from the river with Great Valley mixed riparian forest (61420); and with Great Valley willow scrub (63410) on sites closer to the river that are subject to more severe flooding disturbance. DISTRIBUTION: Formerly extensive along the major low-gradient (depositional) streams throughout the Great Valley, but now reduced to scattered, isolated remnants or young stands because of flood control, water diversion, agricultural development, and urban expansion; typically below about 1,000 feet in the north, 3,000 feet in the south. UPDATE: 10/86. NOTE: *Salix gooddingii* var. *variabilis* listed as characteristic species.

Great Valley Mixed Riparian Forest (61420)

This is a tall, dense, winter-deciduous, broadleafed riparian forest. The tree canopy is usually fairly well closed and moderately to densely stocked with several species including *Acer negundo, Juglans hindsii, Platanus racemosa, Populus fremontii, Salix gooddingii, Salix laevigata,* and *Salix lucida.* Understories consist of these taxa plus shade-tolerant shrubs like *Cephalanthus occidentalis* and *Fraxinus latifolia.* Several lianas are conspicuous in both tree and shrub canopies. SITE FACTORS: Relatively fine-textured alluvium somewhat back from active river channels. These sites experience overbank flooding (with abundant alluvial deposition and groundwater recharge) but not too severe physical battering or erosion. Intergrades closer to the river with Great Valley cottonwood riparian forest (61410) where disturbance is both more frequent and more severe; intergrades farther away from the river with Great Valley oak riparian forest (61430) where such disturbance is less. DISTRIBUTION: Floodplains of low-gradient, depositional streams of the Great Valley, usually below about 500 feet. Formerly very extensive in the Sacramento and northern San Joaquin Valleys, this forest largely has been cleared for agriculture, flood control, and urban expansion. UPDATE: 10/86. NOTE: *Salix gooddingii* var. *variabilis* listed as characteristic species.

Great Valley Oak Riparian Forest (61430)

A medium to tall (rarely to 100 feet), broadleafed, winter-deciduous, closed-canopy riparian forest dominated by *Quercus lobata*. Understories include scattered *Fraxinus latifolia, Juglans hindsii*, and *Platanus racemosa* as well as young *Quercus lobata*. Lianas are often conspicuous, quickly occupying wind-throw generated light gaps. They also are more scattered throughout the shady understory. SITE FACTORS: Restricted to the highest parts of floodplains, most distant from or higher above active river channels and therefore less subject to physical disturbance from flooding, but still receiving annual inputs of silty alluvium and subsurface irrigation. Intergrades closer to the river with Great Valley mixed riparian forest (61420). DISTRIBUTION: Formerly extensive on low-gradient, depositional reaches of the major streams of the Sacramento and northern San Joaquin Valleys. More scattered in the San Joaquin watershed and on the floodplains of the Kings and Kaweah Rivers. Now virtually eliminated by agriculture and firewood harvesting. UPDATE: 10/86

Great Valley Willow Scrub (63410)

An open to dense, broadleafed, winter-deciduous shrubby streamside thicket dominated by any of several *Salix* species. Dense stands usually have little understory or herbaceous component. More open stands have grassy understories, usually dominated by introduced species. DISTRIBUTION: Along all of the major rivers and most of the smaller streams throughout the Great Valley watershed, usually below 1,000 feet. UPDATE: 10/86

GRASSLAND CLASSIFICATIONS

Non-Native Grassland (42200)

A dense to sparse cover of annual grasses reaching up to 3 feet in height. This grassland is often associated with numerous species of showy-flowered, native annual forbs (wildflowers), especially in years of favorable rainfall. Germination occurs with the onset of late fall rains. Growth, flowering, and seed-set occur from winter through spring. With few exceptions, the plants are dead through the summer and fall dry season, and persist as seeds. SITE FACTORS: On fine-textured, usually clay soils, moist or even waterlogged during the winter rainy season and very dry during the summer and fall. Oak woodland (71100) is often adjacent on more moist and better drained soils. DISTRIBUTION: Valleys and foothills throughout most of California, except for the north coastal and desert regions. Usually below 3,000 feet, but can occur up to 4,000 feet in the Tehachapi Mountains and interior San Diego County. Intergrades with portions of the Sacramento, San Joaquin, and Salinas Valleys as well as the Los Angeles Basin, areas that are now agricultural or urban. UPDATE: 10/86.

WETLAND CLASSIFICATION

Coastal and Valley Freshwater Marsh (52410)

Dominated by perennial, emergent monocots to 4–5 m tall. Often forming completely closed canopies. *Scirpus* and *Typha* dominated types and their environmental and floristic distinctions require clarification. SITE FACTORS: Quiet sites (lacking significant current) permanently flooded by fresh water (rather than brackish, alkaline, or variable). Prolonged saturation permits accumulation of deep, peaty soils. DISTRIBUTION: Occasional along the coast and in coastal valleys near river mouths and around the margins of lakes and springs. Most extensive in the upper portion of the Sacramento-San Joaquin River Delta. Common in the Sacramento and San Joaquin Valleys in river oxbows and other areas on the flood plain. Occasional along the Colorado River on the California-Arizona border. Now much reduced in area through its entire range. UPDATE: 10/86. NOTE: Holland questions whether *Typha angustifolia* is a characteristic species.

APPENDIX B. COMMON AND SCIENTIFIC NAMES OF SPECIES APPEARING IN THE TEXT

Table B-1. Common and Scientific Names of Plant Species Identified in the SRNWR Draft EA

Common Name	Scientific Name
adobe-lily	*Fritillaria pluriflora*
alkali milk-vetch	*Astragalus tener* var. *tener*
blackberries	*Rubus* spp.
blue elderberry	*Sambucus mexicana*
blue wildrye	*Elymus glaucus*
box elder	*Acer negundo*
button-brush	*Cephalanthus occidentalis*
California blackberry	*Rubus vitifolius*
California wild grape	*Vitis californica*
California wild rose	*Rosa californica*
cattail	*Typha* spp.
Colusa grass	*Neostapfia colusana*
coyote brush	*Baccharis pilularis*
deergrass	*Matzlenbergia rigens*
dwarf downingia	*Downingia pusilla*
Ferris's milk vetch	*Astragalus tener* var. *ferrisiae*
four-angled spikerush	*Eleocharis quadrangulata*
fox sedge	*Carex vulpinoidea*
Fremont cottonwood	*Populus fremontii*
meadow barley	*Hordeum brachyantherum*
mule fat	*Baccharis viminea*
Oregon ash	*Fraxinus latifolia*
purple needlegrass	*Nassella pulcra*
Red Bluff dwarf rush	*Juncus leiospermus* var. *leiospermus*
rose-mallow a.k.a. California hibiscus	*Hibiscus lasiocarpus*
Santa Barbara sedge	*carex barbarae*
silky cryptantha	*Cryptantha crinita*
valley oak	*Quercus lobata*
western sycamore	*Platanus racemosa*
white alder	*Alnus rhombifolia*
wildrye	*Leymus triticoides*
willows	*Salix* spp.

Table B-2. Common and Scientific Names of Wildlife and Fish Species Identified in the SRNWR Draft EA

Common Name	Scientific Name
Aleutian Canada goose	*Branta canadensis leucopareia*
American avocet	*Recurvirostra americana*
American badger	*Taxidae taxus*
American goldfinch	*Carduelis tristis*
American peregrine falcon	*Falco peregrinus anatum*
American shad	*Alosa sapidissima*
American white pelican	*Pelecanus erythrorhynchos*
American wigeon	*Anas americana*
Audubon cottontail (desert cottontail)	*Sylvilagus audubani*
bald eagle	*Haliaeetus leucocephalus*
bank swallow	*Riparia riparia*
black crappie	*Pomoxis nigromaculatus*
black-necked stilt	*Himantopus mexicanus*
black-tailed deer	*Odocoileus hemionus*
black-tailed hare	*Lepus californicus*
black tern	*Chlidonias niger*
bluegill	*Lepomis macrochirus*
Botta's pocket gopher	*Thomomys bottae*
Brewer's blackbird	*Euphagus cyanocephalus*
brown bullhead	*Ictalurus nebulosus*
brown trout	*Salmo trutta*
Bullock's oriole	*Icterus bullockii*
California horned lizard	*Phrynosoma coronatum frontale*
California vole	*Microtus californicus*
California red-legged frog	*Rana aurora draytonii*
California tiger salamander	*Ambystoma californiense (=A. tigrinum c.)*
California yellow warbler	*Dendroica petechia brewsteri*
Central Valley steelhead	*Oncorhynchus mykiss*
channel catfish	*Ictalurus punctatus*
chinook salmon	*Oncorhynchus tshawytscha*
common yellowthroat	*Geothlypis trichas*
Cooper's hawk	*Accipiter cooperii*
deer mouse	*Peromyscus maniculatus*
double-crested cormorant	*Phalacrocorax auritus*
dowitcher	*Limnodromus*
dunlin	*Calidris alpina*
European starling	*Sturnus vulgaris*
fall-run chinook salmon	*Oncorhynchus tshawytscha*

Common Name	Scientific Name
giant garter snake	*Thamnophis gigas*
golden eagle	*Aquila chrysaetos*
golden shiner	*Notemigonus crysaleucas*
great egret	*Ardea alba*
greater sandhill crane	*Grus canadensis tabida*
green sturgeon	*Acipenser medirostris*
green sunfish	*Lepomois cyanellus*
green-winged teal	*Anas crecca*
house finch	*Carpodacus mexicanus*
largemouth bass	*Micropterus salmoides*
late fall-run chinook	*Oncorhynchus mykiss*
lazuli bunting	*passerina amoena*
least bittern	*Ixobrychus exilis*
least sandpiper	*Calidris minutilla*
loggerhead shrike	*Lanius ludovicianus*
long-billed curlew	*Numenius americanus*
long-eared owl	*Asio otus*
mallard	*Anas platyrhynchos*
Merlin	*Falco columbarius*
mountain plover	*Charadrius montanus*
mourning dove	*Zenaida macroura*
northern harrier	*Circus cyaneus*
northern pintail	*Anas acuta*
northern shoveler	*Anas clypeata*
northwestern pond turtle	*Clemmys marmorata marmorata*
Norway rat	*Rattus norvegicus*
Nuttall's woodpecker	*Picoides nuttallii*
osprey	*Pandion haliaetus*
Pacific chorus frogs	*Hyla regilla*
Pacific gopher snake	*Pituophis melanoleucus catenifer*
pacific lamprey	*Lampetra tridentata*
Pale Townsend's (=western) big-eared bat	*Corynorhinus townsendii pallescens*
Pallid bat	*Antrozous pallidus*
pocket gopher	*Thomomys bottae*
prairie falcon	*Falco mexicanus*
purple martin	*Progne subis*
rainbow trout (steelhead)	*Oncorhynchus mykiss*
red-winged blackbird	*Agelaius phoeniceus*

Common Name	Scientific Name
ring-billed gull	*Larus delawarensis*
ringtail	*Basariscus astutas*
Sacramento splittail	*Pogonichthys macrolepidotus*
Sacramento squawfish	*Ptychocheilus grandis*
Sacramento sucker	*Catostomus occidentalis*
western scrub-jay	*Aphelocoma californica*
sharp-shinned hawk	*Accipiter striatus*
short-eared owl	*Asio flammeus*
snowy egret	*Egretta thula*
song sparrow	*Melospiza melodia*
spotted towhee	*Pipilo maculatus*
spring-run chinook salmon	*Oncorhynchus tshawytscha*
steelhead	*Oncorhynchus mykiss*
striped bass	*Morone saxatilis*
striped skunk	*Mephitis mephitis*
Swainson's hawk	*Buteo swainsoni*
tree swallow	*Tachycineta bicolor*
tricolored blackbird	*Agelaius tricolor*
valley elderberry longhorn beetle	*Desmocerus californicus dimorphus*
vernal pool fairy shrimp	*Branchinecta lynchi*
vernal pool tadpole shrimp	*Lepidurus packardi*
western bluebird	*Sialia mexicana*
western burrowing owl	*Athene cunicularia hypugea*
western fence lizard	*Sceloporus occidentalis*
western harvest mouse	*Reithrodontomys megalotis*
western kingbird	*Tyrannus verticalis*
western sandpiper	*Calidris mauri*
western spadefoot	*Scaphiopus hammondii*
western yellow-billed cuckoo	*Coccyzus americanus occidentalis*
white catfish	*Ictalurus catus*
white crappie	*Pomoxis annularis*
white-faced ibis	*Plegadis chihi*
white-fronted goose	*Anser albifrons*
white sturgeon	*Acipenser transmontanus*
white-tailed kite	*Elanus leucurus*
willow flycatcher	*Empidonax traillii*
winter-run chinook salmon	*Oncorhynchus tshawytscha*
yellow-breasted chat	*Icteria virens*

APPENDIX C. U.S. FISH AND WILDLIFE
SERVICE SPECIES LIST

United States Department of the Interior

FISH AND WILDLIFE SERVICE
Sacramento Fish and Wildlife Office
2800 Cottage Way, Room W-2605
Sacramento, California 95825-1846

IN REPLY REFER TO
1-1-01-SP-831

January 22, 2001

Ms. Allison Fisher
Jones and Stokes Associates
2600 V Street, Suite 100
Sacramento, California 95818-1914

      Subject: Species List for Environmental Assessment for the Sacramento River
                   National Wildlife Refuge, California

Dear Ms. Fisher:

We are sending the enclosed list in response to your January 22, 2001, request for information
about endangered and threatened species (Enclosure A). The list covers the following U.S.
Geological Survey 7½ minute quad or quads: Butte City, Princeton, Ord Ferry, Llano Seco, Red
Bluff East, and Los Molinos Quads.

Please read *Important Information About Your Species List* (enclosed). It explains how we made
the list and describes your responsibilities under the Endangered Species Act. Please contact
Harry Mossman, Biological Technician, at (916) 414-6674, if you have any questions about the
attached list or your responsibilities under the Endangered Species Act. For the fastest response
to species list requests, address them to the attention of Mr. Mossman at this address. You may
fax requests to him at 414-6712 or 6713.

                Sincerely,

                Karen J. Miller
                Chief, Endangered Species Division

Enclosures

ENCLOSURE A

Endangered and Threatened Species that May Occur in or be Affected by
Projects in the Area of the Following California Counties
Reference File No. 1-1-01-SP-831
January 22, 2001

BUTTE COUNTY

Listed Species

Birds

Aleutian Canada goose, *Branta canadensis leucopareia* (T)

bald eagle, *Haliaeetus leucocephalus* (T)

Reptiles

giant garter snake, *Thamnophis gigas* (T)

Amphibians

California red-legged frog, *Rana aurora draytonii* (T)

Fish

Critical habitat, winter-run chinook salmon, *Oncorhynchus tshawytscha* (E)

winter-run chinook salmon, *Oncorhynchus tshawytscha* (E)

delta smelt, *Hypomesus transpacificus* (T)

Central Valley steelhead, *Oncorhynchus mykiss* (T)

Central Valley spring-run chinook salmon, *Oncorhynchus tshawytscha* (T)

Critical Habitat, Central Valley spring-run chinook, *Oncorhynchus tshawytscha* (T)

Sacramento splittail, *Pogonichthys macrolepidotus* (T)

Invertebrates

Conservancy fairy shrimp, *Branchinecta conservatio* (E)

vernal pool tadpole shrimp, *Lepidurus packardi* (E)

vernal pool fairy shrimp, *Branchinecta lynchi* (T)

valley elderberry longhorn beetle, *Desmocerus californicus dimorphus* (T)

Plants

Butte County (Shippee) meadowfoam, *Limnanthes floccosa ssp. californica* (E)

hairy Orcutt grass, *Orcuttia pilosa* (E)

Greene's tuctoria, *Tuctoria greenei* (E)

Hoover's spurge, *Chamaesyce hooveri* (T)

Candidate Species

Fish

Central Valley fall/late fall-run chinook salmon, *Oncorhynchus tshawytscha* (C)

Species of Concern

Mammals

pale Townsend's big-eared bat, *Corynorhinus (=Plecotus) townsendii pallescens* (SC)

Pacific western big-eared bat, *Corynorhinus (=Plecotus) townsendii townsendii* (SC)

Marysville Heermann's kangaroo rat, *Dipodomys californicus eximius* (SC)

spotted bat, *Euderma maculatum* (SC)

greater western mastiff-bat, *Eumops perotis californicus* (SC)

Sierra Nevada snowshoe hare, *Lepus americanus tahoensis* (SC)

Pacific fisher, *Martes pennanti pacifica* (SC)

small-footed myotis bat, *Myotis ciliolabrum* (SC)

long-eared myotis bat, *Myotis evotis* (SC)

fringed myotis bat, *Myotis thysanodes* (SC)

long-legged myotis bat, *Myotis volans* (SC)

Yuma myotis bat, *Myotis yumanensis* (SC)

San Joaquin pocket mouse, *Perognathus inornatus* (SC)

Birds

Swainson's hawk, *Buteo Swainsoni* (CA)

little willow flycatcher, *Empidonax traillii brewsteri* (CA)

greater sandhill crane, *Grus canadensis tabida* (CA)

bank swallow, *Riparia riparia* (CA)

American peregrine falcon, *Falco peregrinus anatum* (D)

Black-Crowned Night Heron, *Nycticorax nycticorax* (MB)

northern goshawk, *Accipiter gentilis* (SC)

tricolored blackbird, *Agelaius tricolor* (SC)

grasshopper sparrow, *Ammodramus savannarum* (SC)

short-eared owl, *Asio flammeus* (SC)

western burrowing owl, *Athene cunicularia hypugea* (SC)

American bittern, *Botaurus lentiginosus* (SC)

ferruginous hawk, *Buteo regalis* (SC)

Lawrence's goldfinch, *Carduelis lawrencei* (SC)

Vaux's swift, *Chaetura vauxi* (SC)

black tern, *Chlidonias niger* (SC)

lark sparrow, *Chondestes grammacus* (SC)

olive-sided flycatcher, *Contopus cooperi* (SC)

black swift, *Cypseloides niger* (SC)

hermit warbler, *Dendroica occidentalis* (SC)

loggerhead shrike, *Lanius ludovicianus* (SC)

Lewis' woodpecker, *Melanerpes lewis* (SC)

white-faced ibis, *Plegadis chihi* (SC)

rufous hummingbird, *Selasphorus rufus* (SC)

red-breasted sapsucker, *Sphyrapicus ruber* (SC)

Brewer's sparrow, *Spizella breweri* (SC)

California spotted owl, *Strix occidentalis occidentalis* (SC)

Bewick's wren, *Thryomanes bewickii* (SC)

Reptiles

    northwestern pond turtle, *Clemmys marmorata marmorata* (SC)

    San Joaquin coachwhip (=whipsnake), *Masticophis flagellum ruddocki* (SC)

    California horned lizard, *Phrynosoma coronatum frontale* (SC)

Amphibians

    foothill yellow-legged frog, *Rana boylii* (SC)

    Cascades frog, *Rana cascadae* (SC)

    mountain yellow-legged frog, *Rana muscosa* (SC)

    western spadefoot toad, *Scaphiopus hammondii* (SC)

Fish

    green sturgeon, *Acipenser medirostris* (SC)

    river lamprey, *Lampetra ayresi* (SC)

    longfin smelt, *Spirinchus thaleichthys* (SC)

Invertebrates

    Sacramento anthicid beetle, *Anthicus sacramento* (SC)

    Sacramento Valley tiger beetle, *Cicindela hirticollis abrupta* (SC)

    California linderiella fairy shrimp, *Linderiella occidentalis* (SC)

Plants

    Jepson's onion, *Allium jepsonii* (SC)

    Ferris's milk-vetch, *Astragalus tener var. ferrisiae* (SC)

    heartscale, *Atriplex cordulata* (SC)

    upswept moonwort, *Botrychium ascendens* (SC)

    scalloped moonwort, *Botrychium crenulatum* (SC)

    Butte County morning-glory, *Calystegia atriplicifolia ssp. buttensis* (SC)

    Mosquin's clarkia, *Clarkia mosquinii ssp. mosquinii* (SC)

    Enterprise clarkia, *Clarkia mosquinii ssp. xerophila* (SC)

    clustered lady's-slipper, *Cypripedium fasciculatum* (SC)

    Butte fritillary, *Fritillaria eastwoodiae* (SC)

    adobe lily, *Fritillaria pluriflora* (SC)

    Ahart's rush, *Juncus leiospermus var. ahartii* (SC)

    veiny monardella, *Monardella douglasii ssp. venosa* (SC)

    little mousetail, *Myosurus minimus ssp. apus* (SC)

    Ahart's whitlow-wort, *Paronychia ahartii* (SC)

    closed-lip (closed-throated) beardtongue, *Penstemon personatus* (SC)

    California beaked-rush, *Rhynchospora californica* (SC)

    valley sagittaria, *Sagittaria sanfordii* (SC)

    Tracy's sanicle, *Sanicula tracyi* (SC)

    Butte County sidalcea, *Sidalcea robusta* (SC)

    Butte County (western) catchfly, *Silene occidentalis ssp. longistipitata* (SC)

TEHAMA COUNTY

Listed Species

Birds

> Aleutian Canada goose, *Branta canadensis leucopareia* (T)
>
> bald eagle, *Haliaeetus leucocephalus* (T)
>
> Critical habitat, northern spotted owl, *Strix occidentalis caurina* (T)
>
> northern spotted owl, *Strix occidentalis caurina* (T)

Reptiles

> giant garter snake, *Thamnophis gigas* (T)

Amphibians

> California red-legged frog, *Rana aurora draytonii* (T)

Fish

> Critical habitat, winter-run chinook salmon, *Oncorhynchus tshawytscha* (E)
>
> winter-run chinook salmon, *Oncorhynchus tshawytscha* (E)
>
> delta smelt, *Hypomesus transpacificus* (T)
>
> Central Valley steelhead, *Oncorhynchus mykiss* (T)
>
> Central Valley spring-run chinook salmon, *Oncorhynchus tshawytscha* (T)
>
> Critical Habitat, Central Valley spring-run chinook, *Oncorhynchus tshawytscha* (T)
>
> Sacramento splittail, *Pogonichthys macrolepidotus* (T)

Invertebrates

> Conservancy fairy shrimp, *Branchinecta conservatio* (E)
>
> vernal pool tadpole shrimp, *Lepidurus packardi* (E)
>
> vernal pool fairy shrimp, *Branchinecta lynchi* (T)
>
> valley elderberry longhorn beetle, *Desmocerus californicus dimorphus* (T)

Plants

> hairy Orcutt grass, *Orcuttia pilosa* (E)
>
> Greene's tuctoria, *Tuctoria greenei* (E)
>
> Hoover's spurge, *Chamaesyce hooveri* (T)
>
> slender Orcutt grass, *Orcuttia tenuis* (T)

Candidate Species

Fish

> Klamath Mts. Province steelhead, *Oncorhynchus mykiss* (C)
>
> Central Valley fall/late fall-run chinook salmon, *Oncorhynchus tshawytscha* (C)

Species of Concern

Mammals

> California wolverine, *Gulo gulo luteus* (CA)
>
> Sierra Nevada red fox, *Vulpes vulpes necator* (CA)
>
> pale Townsend's big-eared bat, *Corynorhinus (=Plecotus) townsendii pallescens* (SC)

Pacific western big-eared bat, *Corynorhinus (=Plecotus) townsendii townsendii* (SC)

spotted bat, *Euderma maculatum* (SC)

Sierra Nevada snowshoe hare, *Lepus americanus tahoensis* (SC)

Pacific fisher, *Martes pennanti pacifica* (SC)

small-footed myotis bat, *Myotis ciliolabrum* (SC)

long-eared myotis bat, *Myotis evotis* (SC)

fringed myotis bat, *Myotis thysanodes* (SC)

long-legged myotis bat, *Myotis volans* (SC)

Yuma myotis bat, *Myotis yumanensis* (SC)

San Joaquin pocket mouse, *Perognathus inornatus* (SC)

Birds

Swainson's hawk, *Buteo Swainsoni* (CA)

little willow flycatcher, *Empidonax traillii brewsteri* (CA)

greater sandhill crane, *Grus canadensis tabida* (CA)

bank swallow, *Riparia riparia* (CA)

American peregrine falcon, *Falco peregrinus anatum* (D)

Black-Crowned Night Heron, *Nycticorax nycticorax* (MB)

northern goshawk, *Accipiter gentilis* (SC)

tricolored blackbird, *Agelaius tricolor* (SC)

grasshopper sparrow, *Ammodramus savannarum* (SC)

Bell's sage sparrow, *Amphispiza belli belli* (SC)

short-eared owl, *Asio flammeus* (SC)

western burrowing owl, *Athene cunicularia hypugea* (SC)

American bittern, *Botaurus lentiginosus* (SC)

ferruginous hawk, *Buteo regalis* (SC)

Lawrence's goldfinch, *Carduelis lawrencei* (SC)

Vaux's swift, *Chaetura vauxi* (SC)

black tern, *Chlidonias niger* (SC)

lark sparrow, *Chondestes grammacus* (SC)

black swift, *Cypseloides niger* (SC)

hermit warbler, *Dendroica occidentalis* (SC)

white-tailed (=black shouldered) kite, *Elanus leucurus* (SC)

loggerhead shrike, *Lanius ludovicianus* (SC)

Lewis' woodpecker, *Melanerpes lewis* (SC)

long-billed curlew, *Numenius americanus* (SC)

white-faced ibis, *Plegadis chihi* (SC)

rufous hummingbird, *Selasphorus rufus* (SC)

Brewer's sparrow, *Spizella breweri* (SC)

California spotted owl, *Strix occidentalis occidentalis* (SC)

Bewick's wren, *Thryomanes bewickii* (SC)

Reptiles

    northwestern pond turtle, *Clemmys marmorata marmorata* (SC)

    California horned lizard, *Phrynosoma coronatum frontale* (SC)

Amphibians

    tailed frog, *Ascaphus truei* (SC)

    foothill yellow-legged frog, *Rana boylii* (SC)

    mountain yellow-legged frog, *Rana muscosa* (SC)

    western spadefoot toad, *Scaphiopus hammondii* (SC)

Fish

    green sturgeon, *Acipenser medirostris* (SC)

    river lamprey, *Lampetra ayresi* (SC)

    longfin smelt, *Spirinchus thaleichthys* (SC)

Invertebrates

    Antioch Dunes anthicid beetle, *Anthicus antiochensis* (SC)

    Sacramento anthicid beetle, *Anthicus sacramento* (SC)

    Leech's skyline diving beetle, *Hydroporus leechi* (SC)

    California linderiella fairy shrimp, *Linderiella occidentalis* (SC)

Plants

    Indian Valley brodiaea, *Brodiaea coronaria ssp. rosea* (CA)

    upswept moonwort, *Botrychium ascendens* (SC)

    scalloped moonwort, *Botrychium crenulatum* (SC)

    Wilkins' harebell, *Campanula wilkinsiana* (SC)

    silky cryptantha, *Cryptantha crinita* (SC)

    clustered lady's-slipper, *Cypripedium fasciculatum* (SC)

    Oregon fireweed, *Epilobium oreganum* (SC)

    Brandegee's woolly-star, *Eriastrum brandegeae* (SC)

    Butte fritillary, *Fritillaria eastwoodiae* (SC)

    adobe lily, *Fritillaria pluriflora* (SC)

    Tehama dwarf-flax, *Hesperolinon tehamense* (SC)

    legenere, *Legenere limosa* (SC)

    Mt. Tedoc linanthus, *Linanthus nuttallii ssp. howellii* (SC)

    red-flowered lotus, *Lotus rubriflorus* (SC)

    Anthony Peak lupine, *Lupinus antoninus* (SC)

    Stebbins' madia, *Madia stebbinsii* (SC)

    The Lassics sandwort, *Minuartia decumbens* (SC)

    Ahart's whitlow-wort, *Paronychia ahartii* (SC)

    valley sagittaria, *Sagittaria sanfordii* (SC)

    Tracy's sanicle, *Sanicula tracyi* (SC)

    Butte County (western) catchfly, *Silene occidentalis ssp. longistipitata* (SC)

KEY:

(E)	*Endangered*	Listed (in the Federal Register) as being in danger of extinction.
(T)	*Threatened*	Listed as likely to become endangered within the foreseeable future.
(P)	*Proposed*	Officially proposed (in the Federal Register) for listing as endangered or threatened.
(PX)	*Proposed Critical Habitat*	Proposed as an area essential to the conservation of the species.
(C)	*Candidate*	Candidate to become a *proposed* species.
(SC)	*Species of Concern*	Other species of concern to the Service.
(D)	*Delisted*	Delisted. Status to be monitored for 5 years.
(CA)	*State-Listed*	Listed as threatened or endangered by the State of California.
*	*Extirpated*	Possibly extirpated from the area.
**	*Extinct*	Possibly extinct
	Critical Habitat	Area essential to the conservation of a species.

Endangered and Threatened Species that May Occur in
or be Affected by Projects in the Selected Quads Listed Below
Reference File No. 1-1-01-SP-831
January 22, 2001

QUAD : 561B   BUTTE CITY

Listed Species

Birds

Aleutian Canada goose, *Branta canadensis leucopareia* (T)

bald eagle, *Haliaeetus leucocephalus* (T)

Reptiles

giant garter snake, *Thamnophis gigas* (T)

Fish

delta smelt, *Hypomesus transpacificus* (T)

Central Valley steelhead, *Oncorhynchus mykiss* (T)

winter-run chinook salmon, *Oncorhynchus tshawytscha* (E)

Central Valley spring-run chinook salmon, *Oncorhynchus tshawytscha* (T)

Critical Habitat, Central Valley spring-run chinook, *Oncorhynchus tshawytscha* (T)

Sacramento splittail, *Pogonichthys macrolepidotus* (T)

Invertebrates

Conservancy fairy shrimp, *Branchinecta conservatio* (E)

vernal pool fairy shrimp, *Branchinecta lynchi* (T)

valley elderberry longhorn beetle, *Desmocerus californicus dimorphus* (T)

vernal pool tadpole shrimp, *Lepidurus packardi* (E)

Candidate Species

Fish

Central Valley fall/late fall-run chinook salmon, *Oncorhynchus tshawytscha* (C)

Species of Concern

Mammals

pale Townsend's big-eared bat, *Corynorhinus (=Plecotus) townsendii pallescens* (SC)

Pacific western big-eared bat, *Corynorhinus (=Plecotus) townsendii townsendii* (SC)

Marysville Heermann's kangaroo rat, *Dipodomys californicus eximius* (SC)

small-footed myotis bat, *Myotis ciliolabrum* (SC)

long-eared myotis bat, *Myotis evotis* (SC)

fringed myotis bat, *Myotis thysanodes* (SC)

long-legged myotis bat, *Myotis volans* (SC)

Yuma myotis bat, *Myotis yumanensis* (SC)

San Joaquin pocket mouse, *Perognathus inornatus* (SC)

Birds

tricolored blackbird, *Agelaius tricolor* (SC)

western burrowing owl, *Athene cunicularia hypugea* (SC)

Swainson's hawk, *Buteo Swainsoni* (CA)

ferruginous hawk, *Buteo regalis* (SC)

little willow flycatcher, *Empidonax traillii brewsteri* (CA)

American peregrine falcon, *Falco peregrinus anatum* (D)

greater sandhill crane, *Grus canadensis tabida* (CA)

white-faced ibis, *Plegadis chihi* (SC)

bank swallow, *Riparia riparia* (CA)

Reptiles

northwestern pond turtle, *Clemmys marmorata marmorata* (SC)

Amphibians

western spadefoot toad, *Scaphiopus hammondii* (SC)

Fish

green sturgeon, *Acipenser medirostris* (SC)

river lamprey, *Lampetra ayresi* (SC)

Pacific lamprey, *Lampetra tridentata* (SC)

longfin smelt, *Spirinchus thaleichthys* (SC)

Invertebrates

Antioch Dunes anthicid beetle, *Anthicus antiochensis* (SC)

Sacramento anthicid beetle, *Anthicus sacramento* (SC)

California linderiella fairy shrimp, *Linderiella occidentalis* (SC)

Plants

Ferris's milk-vetch, *Astragalus tener var. ferrisiae* (SC)

QUAD : 562A   PRINCETON

Listed Species

Birds

Aleutian Canada goose, *Branta canadensis leucopareia* (T)

bald eagle, *Haliaeetus leucocephalus* (T)

northern spotted owl, *Strix occidentalis caurina* (T)

Reptiles

giant garter snake, *Thamnophis gigas* (T)

Fish

delta smelt, *Hypomesus transpacificus* (T)

Central Valley steelhead, *Oncorhynchus mykiss* (T)

Critical habitat, winter-run chinook salmon, *Oncorhynchus tshawytscha* (E)

winter-run chinook salmon, *Oncorhynchus tshawytscha* (E)

Central Valley spring-run chinook salmon, *Oncorhynchus tshawytscha* (T)

Critical Habitat, Central Valley spring-run chinook, *Oncorhynchus tshawytscha* (T)

Sacramento splittail, *Pogonichthys macrolepidotus* (T)

Invertebrates

Conservancy fairy shrimp, *Branchinecta conservatio* (E)

vernal pool fairy shrimp, *Branchinecta lynchi* (T)

valley elderberry longhorn beetle, *Desmocerus californicus dimorphus* (T)

vernal pool tadpole shrimp, *Lepidurus packardi* (E)

Plants

Colusa grass, *Neostapfia colusana* (T) *

Candidate Species

Fish

Central Valley fall/late fall-run chinook salmon, *Oncorhynchus tshawytscha* (C)

Species of Concern

Mammals

Pacific western big-eared bat, *Corynorhinus (=Plecotus) townsendii townsendii* (SC)

Marysville Heermann's kangaroo rat, *Dipodomys californicus eximius* (SC)

small-footed myotis bat, *Myotis ciliolabrum* (SC)

long-eared myotis bat, *Myotis evotis* (SC)

fringed myotis bat, *Myotis thysanodes* (SC)

long-legged myotis bat, *Myotis volans* (SC)

Yuma myotis bat, *Myotis yumanensis* (SC)

San Joaquin pocket mouse, *Perognathus inornatus* (SC)

Birds

tricolored blackbird, *Agelaius tricolor* (SC)

western burrowing owl, *Athene cunicularia hypugea* (SC)

Swainson's hawk, *Buteo Swainsoni* (CA)

    ferruginous hawk, *Buteo regalis* (SC)

    little willow flycatcher, *Empidonax traillii brewsteri* (CA)

    American peregrine falcon, *Falco peregrinus anatum* (D)

    greater sandhill crane, *Grus canadensis tabida* (CA)

    white-faced ibis, *Plegadis chihi* (SC)

    bank swallow, *Riparia riparia* (CA)

Reptiles

    northwestern pond turtle, *Clemmys marmorata marmorata* (SC)

Amphibians

    western spadefoot toad, *Scaphiopus hammondii* (SC)

Fish

    green sturgeon, *Acipenser medirostris* (SC)

    river lamprey, *Lampetra ayresi* (SC)

    Pacific lamprey, *Lampetra tridentata* (SC)

    longfin smelt, *Spirinchus thaleichthys* (SC)

Invertebrates

    Antioch Dunes anthicid beetle, *Anthicus antiochensis* (SC)

    Sacramento anthicid beetle, *Anthicus sacramento* (SC)

    California linderiella fairy shrimp, *Linderiella occidentalis* (SC)

QUAD : 577B   ORD FERRY

Listed Species

Birds

    Aleutian Canada goose, *Branta canadensis leucopareia* (T)

    bald eagle, *Haliaeetus leucocephalus* (T)

Reptiles

    giant garter snake, *Thamnophis gigas* (T)

Amphibians

    California red-legged frog, *Rana aurora draytonii* (T)

Fish

    delta smelt, *Hypomesus transpacificus* (T)

    Central Valley steelhead, *Oncorhynchus mykiss* (T)

    Critical habitat, winter-run chinook salmon, *Oncorhynchus tshawytscha* (E)

    winter-run chinook salmon, *Oncorhynchus tshawytscha* (E)

Central Valley spring-run chinook salmon, *Oncorhynchus tshawytscha* (T)

Sacramento splittail, *Pogonichthys macrolepidotus* (T)

Invertebrates

Conservancy fairy shrimp, *Branchinecta conservatio* (E)

vernal pool fairy shrimp, *Branchinecta lynchi* (T)

valley elderberry longhorn beetle, *Desmocerus californicus dimorphus* (T)

vernal pool tadpole shrimp, *Lepidurus packardi* (E)

Candidate Species

Fish

Central Valley fall/late fall-run chinook salmon, *Oncorhynchus tshawytscha* (C)

Species of Concern

Mammals

pale Townsend's big-eared bat, *Corynorhinus (=Plecotus) townsendii pallescens* (SC)

Pacific western big-eared bat, *Corynorhinus (=Plecotus) townsendii townsendii* (SC)

Marysville Heermann's kangaroo rat, *Dipodomys californicus eximius* (SC)

greater western mastiff-bat, *Eumops perotis californicus* (SC)

small-footed myotis bat, *Myotis ciliolabrum* (SC)

long-eared myotis bat, *Myotis evotis* (SC)

fringed myotis bat, *Myotis thysanodes* (SC)

long-legged myotis bat, *Myotis volans* (SC)

Yuma myotis bat, *Myotis yumanensis* (SC)

San Joaquin pocket mouse, *Perognathus inornatus* (SC)

Birds

western burrowing owl, *Athene cunicularia hypugea* (SC)

Swainson's hawk, *Buteo Swainsoni* (CA)

ferruginous hawk, *Buteo regalis* (SC)

little willow flycatcher, *Empidonax traillii brewsteri* (CA)

American peregrine falcon, *Falco peregrinus anatum* (D)

greater sandhill crane, *Grus canadensis tabida* (CA)

white-faced ibis, *Plegadis chihi* (SC)

bank swallow, *Riparia riparia* (CA)

Reptiles

northwestern pond turtle, *Clemmys marmorata marmorata* (SC)

Amphibians

　　western spadefoot toad, *Scaphiopus hammondii*　(SC)

Fish

　　green sturgeon, *Acipenser medirostris*　(SC)

　　river lamprey, *Lampetra ayresi*　(SC)

　　longfin smelt, *Spirinchus thaleichthys*　(SC)

Invertebrates

　　Antioch Dunes anthicid beetle, *Anthicus antiochensis*　(SC)

　　Sacramento anthicid beetle, *Anthicus sacramento*　(SC)

　　California linderiella fairy shrimp, *Linderiella occidentalis*　(SC)

QUAD : 577C　LLANO SECO

Listed Species

Birds

　　Aleutian Canada goose, *Branta canadensis leucopareia*　(T)

　　bald eagle, *Haliaeetus leucocephalus*　(T)

Reptiles

　　giant garter snake, *Thamnophis gigas*　(T)

Amphibians

　　California red-legged frog, *Rana aurora draytonii*　(T)

Fish

　　delta smelt, *Hypomesus transpacificus*　(T)

　　Central Valley steelhead, *Oncorhynchus mykiss*　(T)

　　Critical habitat, winter-run chinook salmon, *Oncorhynchus tshawytscha*　(E)

　　winter-run chinook salmon, *Oncorhynchus tshawytscha*　(E)

　　Central Valley spring-run chinook salmon, *Oncorhynchus tshawytscha*　(T)

　　Critical Habitat, Central Valley spring-run chinook, *Oncorhynchus tshawytscha*　(T)

　　Sacramento splittail, *Pogonichthys macrolepidotus*　(T)

Invertebrates

　　Conservancy fairy shrimp, *Branchinecta conservatio*　(E)

　　vernal pool fairy shrimp, *Branchinecta lynchi*　(T)

　　valley elderberry longhorn beetle, *Desmocerus californicus dimorphus*　(T)

　　vernal pool tadpole shrimp, *Lepidurus packardi*　(E)

Candidate Species

Fish

Central Valley fall/late fall-run chinook salmon, *Oncorhynchus tshawytscha* (C)

Species of Concern

Mammals

pale Townsend's big-eared bat, *Corynorhinus (=Plecotus) townsendii pallescens* (SC)

Pacific western big-eared bat, *Corynorhinus (=Plecotus) townsendii townsendii* (SC)

Marysville Heermann's kangaroo rat, *Dipodomys californicus eximius* (SC)

greater western mastiff-bat, *Eumops perotis californicus* (SC)

small-footed myotis bat, *Myotis ciliolabrum* (SC)

long-eared myotis bat, *Myotis evotis* (SC)

fringed myotis bat, *Myotis thysanodes* (SC)

long-legged myotis bat, *Myotis volans* (SC)

Yuma myotis bat, *Myotis yumanensis* (SC)

San Joaquin pocket mouse, *Perognathus inornatus* (SC)

Birds

tricolored blackbird, *Agelaius tricolor* (SC)

western burrowing owl, *Athene cunicularia hypugea* (SC)

Swainson's hawk, *Buteo Swainsoni* (CA)

ferruginous hawk, *Buteo regalis* (SC)

little willow flycatcher, *Empidonax traillii brewsteri* (CA)

American peregrine falcon, *Falco peregrinus anatum* (D)

greater sandhill crane, *Grus canadensis tabida* (CA)

white-faced ibis, *Plegadis chihi* (SC)

bank swallow, *Riparia riparia* (CA)

Reptiles

northwestern pond turtle, *Clemmys marmorata marmorata* (SC)

Amphibians

western spadefoot toad, *Scaphiopus hammondii* (SC)

Fish

green sturgeon, *Acipenser medirostris* (SC)

river lamprey, *Lampetra ayresi* (SC)

longfin smelt, *Spirinchus thaleichthys* (SC)

Invertebrates

    Antioch Dunes anthicid beetle, *Anthicus antiochensis* (SC)

    Sacramento anthicid beetle, *Anthicus sacramento* (SC)

    California linderiella fairy shrimp, *Linderiella occidentalis* (SC)

QUAD : 610B   RED BLUFF EAST

Listed Species

Birds

    Aleutian Canada goose, *Branta canadensis leucopareia* (T)

    bald eagle, *Haliaeetus leucocephalus* (T)

Reptiles

    giant garter snake, *Thamnophis gigas* (T)

Amphibians

    California red-legged frog, *Rana aurora draytonii* (T)

Fish

    delta smelt, *Hypomesus transpacificus* (T)

    Central Valley steelhead, *Oncorhynchus mykiss* (T)

    Critical habitat, winter-run chinook salmon, *Oncorhynchus tshawytscha* (E)

    winter-run chinook salmon, *Oncorhynchus tshawytscha* (E)

    Central Valley spring-run chinook salmon, *Oncorhynchus tshawytscha* (T)

    Critical Habitat, Central Valley spring-run chinook, *Oncorhynchus tshawytscha* (T)

    Sacramento splittail, *Pogonichthys macrolepidotus* (T)

Invertebrates

    vernal pool fairy shrimp, *Branchinecta lynchi* (T)

    valley elderberry longhorn beetle, *Desmocerus californicus dimorphus* (T)

    vernal pool tadpole shrimp, *Lepidurus packardi* (E)

Candidate Species

Fish

    Central Valley fall/late fall-run chinook salmon, *Oncorhynchus tshawytscha* (C)

Species of Concern

Mammals

    pale Townsend's big-eared bat, *Corynorhinus (=Plecotus) townsendii pallescens* (SC)

    Pacific western big-eared bat, *Corynorhinus (=Plecotus) townsendii townsendii* (SC)

    spotted bat, *Euderma maculatum* (SC)

small-footed myotis bat, *Myotis ciliolabrum* (SC)

long-eared myotis bat, *Myotis evotis* (SC)

fringed myotis bat, *Myotis thysanodes* (SC)

long-legged myotis bat, *Myotis volans* (SC)

Yuma myotis bat, *Myotis yumanensis* (SC)

San Joaquin pocket mouse, *Perognathus inornatus* (SC)

Birds

western burrowing owl, *Athene cunicularia hypugea* (SC)

Swainson's hawk, *Buteo Swainsoni* (CA)

ferruginous hawk, *Buteo regalis* (SC)

little willow flycatcher, *Empidonax traillii brewsteri* (CA)

American peregrine falcon, *Falco peregrinus anatum* (D)

white-faced ibis, *Plegadis chihi* (SC)

bank swallow, *Riparia riparia* (CA)

Reptiles

northwestern pond turtle, *Clemmys marmorata marmorata* (SC)

Amphibians

foothill yellow-legged frog, *Rana boylii* (SC)

western spadefoot toad, *Scaphiopus hammondii* (SC)

Fish

green sturgeon, *Acipenser medirostris* (SC)

river lamprey, *Lampetra ayresi* (SC)

longfin smelt, *Spirinchus thaleichthys* (SC)

Invertebrates

Antioch Dunes anthicid beetle, *Anthicus antiochensis* (SC)

Sacramento anthicid beetle, *Anthicus sacramento* (SC)

California linderiella fairy shrimp, *Linderiella occidentalis* (SC)

Plants

silky cryptantha, *Cryptantha crinita* (SC)

adobe lily, *Fritillaria pluriflora* (SC)

QUAD : 610D   LOS MOLINOS

Listed Species

Birds

Aleutian Canada goose, *Branta canadensis leucopareia* (T)

bald eagle, *Haliaeetus leucocephalus* (T)

Reptiles

giant garter snake, *Thamnophis gigas* (T)

Amphibians

California red-legged frog, *Rana aurora draytonii* (T)

Fish

delta smelt, *Hypomesus transpacificus* (T)

Central Valley steelhead, *Oncorhynchus mykiss* (T)

winter-run chinook salmon, *Oncorhynchus tshawytscha* (E)

Central Valley spring-run chinook salmon, *Oncorhynchus tshawytscha* (T)

Critical Habitat, Central Valley spring-run chinook, *Oncorhynchus tshawytscha* (T)

Sacramento splittail, *Pogonichthys macrolepidotus* (T)

Invertebrates

Conservancy fairy shrimp, *Branchinecta conservatio* (E)

vernal pool fairy shrimp, *Branchinecta lynchi* (T)

valley elderberry longhorn beetle, *Desmocerus californicus dimorphus* (T)

vernal pool tadpole shrimp, *Lepidurus packardi* (E)

Candidate Species

Fish

Central Valley fall/late fall-run chinook salmon, *Oncorhynchus tshawytscha* (C)

Species of Concern

Mammals

pale Townsend's big-eared bat, *Corynorhinus (=Plecotus) townsendii pallescens* (SC)

Pacific western big-eared bat, *Corynorhinus (=Plecotus) townsendii townsendii* (SC)

spotted bat, *Euderma maculatum* (SC)

small-footed myotis bat, *Myotis ciliolabrum* (SC)

long-eared myotis bat, *Myotis evotis* (SC)

fringed myotis bat, *Myotis thysanodes* (SC)

long-legged myotis bat, *Myotis volans* (SC)

Yuma myotis bat, *Myotis yumanensis* (SC)

San Joaquin pocket mouse, *Perognathus inornatus* (SC)

Birds

western burrowing owl, *Athene cunicularia hypugea* (SC)

ferruginous hawk, *Buteo regalis* (SC)

little willow flycatcher, *Empidonax traillii brewsteri* (CA)

American peregrine falcon, *Falco peregrinus anatum* (D)

white-faced ibis, *Plegadis chihi* (SC)

bank swallow, *Riparia riparia* (CA)

Reptiles

northwestern pond turtle, *Clemmys marmorata marmorata* (SC)

Amphibians

foothill yellow-legged frog, *Rana boylii* (SC)

western spadefoot toad, *Scaphiopus hammondii* (SC)

Fish

green sturgeon, *Acipenser medirostris* (SC)

river lamprey, *Lampetra ayresi* (SC)

longfin smelt, *Spirinchus thaleichthys* (SC)

Invertebrates

Antioch Dunes anthicid beetle, *Anthicus antiochensis* (SC)

Sacramento anthicid beetle, *Anthicus sacramento* (SC)

California linderiella fairy shrimp, *Linderiella occidentalis* (SC)

KEY:

(E)	*Endangered*	Listed (in the Federal Register) as being in danger of extinction.
(T)	*Threatened*	Listed as likely to become endangered within the foreseeable future.
(P)	*Proposed*	Officially proposed (in the Federal Register) for listing as endangered or threatened.
(PX)	*Proposed Critical Habitat*	Proposed as an area essential to the conservation of the species.
(C)	*Candidate*	Candidate to become a *proposed* species.
(SC)	*Species of Concern*	May be endangered or threatened. Not enough biological information has been gathered to support listing at this time.
(MB)	*Migratory Bird*	Migratory bird
(D)	*Delisted*	Delisted. Status to be monitored for 5 years.
(CA)	*State-Listed*	Listed as threatened or endangered by the State of California.
(*)	*Extirpated*	Possibly extirpated from this quad.
(**)	*Extinct*	Possibly extinct.
	Critical Habitat	Area essential to the conservation of a species.

APPENDIX D. DISTRIBUTION LIST

APPENDIX D. DISTRIBUTION LIST FOR ENVIRONMENTAL ASSESSMENT

Federal, State, and County Elected Officials

Office of U.S. Senator Barbara Boxer
Office of U.S. Senator Dianne Feinstein
Office of U.S. Representative Wally Herger
Office of U.S. Representative Doug Ose
Office of State Senator Maurice Johannessen
Office of State Senator Tim Leslie
Office of State Senator Rico Oller
Office of State Assemblyman Sam Aanestad
Office of State Assemblyman Richard Dickerson
Chairperson, Butte County Board of Supervisors
Chairperson, Colusa County Board of Supervisors
Chairperson, Glenn County Board of Supervisors
Chairperson, Tehama County Board of Supervisors

Federal Agencies

U.S. Department of Agriculture
    U.S. Forest Service
        James Fenwood, Forest Supervisor
    Natural Resource Conservation Service - Colusa, Willows
    Dan Martynn, District Conservationist
    Dennis Nay, District Conservationist
U.S. Department of Commerce
    National Marine Fisheries Service
        Mike Aceitano
U.S. Department of Defense
    U.S. Army Corps of Engineers
        Art Champ, Chief, Regulatory Branch
        Steve Yaeger, State Study Manager, Comprehensive Study
        Susan Fry, Comprehensive Study
U.S. Department of the Interior
    Bureau of Reclamation - Sacramento, Red Bluff
        Dan Keppan - Mid Pacific Regional Office
        Basia Trout
    Fish and Wildlife Service - Sacramento, Stockton, Red Bluff, Sherwood, OR
        Wayne White, Field Supervisor

Joel Medlin, Deputy Field Supervisor
Bob Shaffer, Central Valley Habitat Joint Venture
Dan Castleberry, Central Valley Project Improvement Act
Marie Sullivan, Central Valley Project Improvement Act
John Icanberry, Central Valley Project Improvement Act
James G. Smith, Project Leader
Patricia Parker, Fisheries Biologist
Anan Raymond, Cultural Resources Team, Region 1

State Agencies

Department of Fish and Game - Sacramento, Redding, Rancho Cordova, Chico, Willows, Butte City
Diana Jacobs, Deputy Director, Science Advisor
Scott Clemons, Riparian Habitat Program Manager, Wildlife Conservation Board
Terry Mansfield, Wildlife and Inland Fisheries Division
Dan Odenweller, Central Valley Bay Delta Branch
Don Koch, Regional Manager, Region 1
Randy Benthin
Banky Curtis, Regional Manager, Region 2
Ron Bertram, Senior Biologist
Paul Ward, Associate Biologist, Marine Fisheries
Paul Hofmann, Wildlife Biologist
Don Blake, Habitat Supervisor
Department of Parks and Recreation
Kathryn Foley, Supervisor
Woody Elliott, Senior Resource Ecologist
Department of Transportation
Trisha Tillotson, Hydraulics, District 3
Department of Water Resources - Sacramento, Red Bluff
Bob Potter, Deputy Director, State Water Project
Annalena Bronson
Earle Cummings
Stacy Cepello
Koll Buer
Fish and Game Commision
Michael Chrisman, President
Richard T. Thieriot, Member
Office of Historic Preservation
Daniel Abeyta
Resources Agency
Tim Ramirez
Rebecca Fawver

State Board of Reclamation
    Betsy Marchand, President of The Reclamation Board
    Peter Rabbon, General Manager

Local

Butte County Cooperative Extension
    Bill Olsen, Director
Butte County
    J. Michael Madden, Emergency Services
    Bob Townsend, Public Works
Glenn County
    John Benoit, Planning Department
Tehama County
    Ernie Ohlin, Public Works
City of Tehama
    Ron Warner, Mayor

Public Libraries

Bayliss Library
Butte County Library
Colusa County Library - Colusa Branch
Colusa County Library - Princeton Branch
Corning Library
Orland City Library
Tehama County Library - Los Molinos Branch
Tehama County Library - Red Bluff Branch
Willows Public Library

Private Groups and Individuals

Alex Oehler, Field Representative, U.S. Congressman Herger
Rueben Williams, Field Representative, State Assemblyman Aanestad
Kim Davis, Field Representative, State Senator Maurice Johannesson
Jane Dolan, Butte County Supervisor
Forrest Sprague, Glenn County Supervisor
William Borror, Tehama County Supervisor
Serge Birk
Don and Barbara Anderson
Ben Carter
Dan Efseaff, Sacramento River Partners
John Carlon, Sacramento River Partners

Dave Vogel
Les Heringer, M&T Ranch, Inc.
Shirley Lewis
Thomas Kraemer
Carlene C. Mann
Curt Martin
Chuck Crain, Crain Walnut Shelling
Charles Ohm
Dr. Thomas A. Flynn, O.D., Shasta View Farms, LLC
Cecilia Flynn, Shasta View Farms
Walt Stile III
John Merz, Sacramento River Preservation Trust
Jose Puente
Suzanne Gibbs, Big Chico Creek Watershed Alliance
Bill Nichols, Nichols Ranch
Dan Taylor, Executive Director, National Audobon Society, California State Office
Jim Bremner, Bremner Farms
Scott Larrabee, Larrabee Farms
Ron Keyawa, Keyawa Orchard/3-B Ranch
Barbara Vlamis, Director, Butte Environmental Council
Chuck DeJournette
Tom Evans
Brendon Flynn, Pacific Farms
Allan Fulton
Dr. Tom Griggs
Gary W. Kramer
Rick Massa
Bruce McGowan
John and April Senior
Pia Sevelius
John Scott
Bill Waggershauer
Van Tenney, General Manager, Glenn-Colusa Irrigation District
Michael Koehnen, C. F. Koehnen & Sons
Sam Lawson, Project Director, The Nature Conservancy
Dr. Marlyce Meyers, The Nature Conservancy
Mike Roberts, The Nature Conservancy
Dawit Zeleke, The Nature Conservancy
Daryl Peterson, The Nature Conservancy
Robert D. Clark, North Delta Water Agency
Harry L. McQuillen, National Wild Turkey Federation
Lance Boyd, Princeton-Codora Irrigation District
Mark Kimmelshue, Butte Basin Water Users Association
Burt Bundy, Sacramento River Advisory Council
Matt Cowell, Western Canal Water District
Ann Chrisney, Riparian Habitat Joint Venture

Bill Gaines, California Waterfowl Association
Lola Jeffers, Reclamation District No, 1004
Ron Stromstad, Ducks Unlimited
Jason Peltier, Central Valley Project Water Association
Dr. Dawn S. Wilson, Department of Biological Sciences
       California State University, Chico
Dr. David S. Wood, Department of Biological Sciences
       California State University, Chico
Dr. Paul Maslin, Department of Biological Sciences
       California State University, Chico
Dr. David L. Brown, Department of Geosciences
       California State University, Chico
Dr. Donald Holtgrieve, Department of Geography and Planning
       California State University, Chico
Jennifer Rotnem, Sponsored Programs
       California State University, Chico
Chuck Nelson, Geographic Information Center
       California State University, Chico
Eric Larsen, University of California, Davis
Goeff Geupel, Point Reyes Bird Observatory
Greg Elliott, Point Reyes Bird Observatory
Richard Laurson

www.ingramcontent.com/pod-product-compliance
Lightning Source LLC
Chambersburg PA
CBHW081105290526
45795CB00006B/2007